Business Ethics Applied

STUDY GUIDE

Michael L. Richardson and Emily V. Baker
contributing author Karen K. White

Pearson
Custom
Publishing

Cover art by Jack Barrett.

References from the textbook *Ethics Applied*, Edition 3.0, Pearson Custom Publishing, 2000, and *Study Guide Ethics Applied*, Edition 3.0, 2000, Pearson Custom Publishing, are used with permission.

Library of Congress Catalog Card Number: 94-12045
1. Ethics   2. Ethics-History   3. Business Ethics
4. Professional Ethics   5. Science and Ethics   6. Social Ethics

Printed in the United States of America

10 9 8 7 6 5 4 3

This manuscript was supplied camera-ready by the authors.

Please visit our web site at www.pearsoncustom.com

ISBN 0–536–60869-5

BA 992126

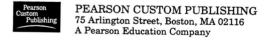

PEARSON CUSTOM PUBLISHING
75 Arlington Street, Boston, MA 02116
A Pearson Education Company

Dedication

To the students, applied ethics faculty, trustees, president, alumni and staff of St. Petersburg Junior College

ACKNOWLEDGMENTS

The contribution in both content and pedagogy of the three primary textbook authors for *Business Ethics Applied* – Dr. Paul DeVries, Dr. Lisa Newton and . Ric S. Machuga – is gratefully acknowledged. Among the many others who played vital roles in both the textbook and Study Guide's creation are Dr. Carl M. Kuttler, Jr., SPJC president, whose vision and commitment made the project possible; trustees including W. Richard Johnston, Chairman; Evelyn Bilirakis, Kenneth P. Burke, Dr. Susan D. Jones, and Kenneth T. Welch. Also involved in the project were past Chairman Dr. Pamela Jo Davis, and former trustees Ann Hines, Lacy Harwell, Robert Young, Stanley A. Brandimore, and Gary Megaloudis, as well as Chairman Emeritus Joseph H. Lang; and Dr. Karen K. White, who guided the establishment of the department and the course and served as textbook project manager and author of the workbook for the first edition. For their contributions and encouragement, the authors also thank the Applied Ethics Faculty at the College including Allen Plunkett, Keith Goree, Lee Miller, Mary Dawn Pyle, JoAnne Hopkins, Tom Derzypolski, Kevin Murray and the Adjunct Faculty.

The Study Guide authors also wish to acknowledge Don Kilburn and David Daniels of Pearson Custom Publishing, and the professional services of publisher's senior editors Hal Hawkins, and JoAnne Weaver, as well as these individuals who assisted in various ways from simple encouragement to detailed editing: Chris Gill, David Henniger, Iris Yetter, Dr. Carol Copenhaver, Kathy Federico, Barbara Barksdale, Shirley Hunter, Dr. Charles Roberts, Kim Corry, Charles Lasater and Margaret Richardson.

TO THE STUDENT

Commonly, an ethics text contains complex subject matter and complex reading materials. Given that reality, what can you do to make sure any time you spend reading the text is to your benefit? You can make sure that your investment in reading pays off. But it will require much more than simply reading the material to comprehend and retain what you read.

Of course, you have only a certain amount of time that you can devote to any reading assignment; also, it is a fact that different instructors use different methods of teaching. This is why you will find numerous suggested strategies in this guide from which you and your instructor may choose in order to assure that your investment in reading *Business Ethics Applied* is useful and efficient.

"General Strategies for Reading *Business Ehics Applied* " appear on the following pages. You may want to choose from these suggestions for reading the text. After the "General Strategies" are sections arranged by chapter, with questions and exercises. As you complete any of these suggested activities, you are engaging in what we call *active reading*, which means you are using critical thinking skills that will help you comprehend and retain the material in the textbook.

It is important to understand that we go through different thinking processes. In fact, Benjamin S. Bloom in his *Taxonomy of Educational Objectives: Cognitive Domain,* Longman, Inc., New York (1956) identifies what we do in the thinking process as:

[1] Knowledge. The ability to bring into mind specific material. Learning activities at this level include outlining, memorizing, reciting, listing, naming and identifying.

[2] Comprehension. The ability to make use of the ideas contained in a reading selection without relating it to other ideas or materials. Learning activities at this level include describing, summarizing, explaining and classifying.

[3] Application. The ability to absorb a new idea, principle or theory and use it in a new situation. Learning activities at this level include applying, drawing, using and solving.

[4] Analysis. The ability to break down material into parts and to detect the relationship of the parts. Learning activities at this level include comparing, contrasting, differentiating, organizing and detecting cause and effect.

[5] Synthesis. The ability to assemble elements or parts to form a whole. Learning activities at this level include creating, designing, constructing and predicting.

[6] Evaluation. The ability to make judgments by using appropriate criteria. Learning activities at this level include arguing, judging, evaluating and appraising.

No one expects you to undertake all of the strategies and exercises for all of your reading assignments. However, it is strongly recommended that you take an opportunity to consider the various suggestions offered, in order to make use of the ones that promise to be most helpful to you in reading the textbook and studying applied ethics.

GENERAL STRATEGIES FOR THE <u>ACTIVE READING</u>
OF
BUSINESS ETHICS APPLIED

The following strategies are adapted from materials and suggestions provided by Mary Gaier, Program Director, Communications Department, Clearwater Campus, St. Petersburg Junior College:

A.   Estimate the amount of time you will need to accomplish the reading assignment. Set time aside accordingly. (See Guide for class and study time at the end of these strategies.)

B.   Use a highlighter; underline; make notes in the margins. Use Post-it notes or other materials as "flags" in order to be able to locate material you have already read more quickly.

C.   Consider using various colors of pens and-or highlighters. Devise your own system; for example:
>   Yellow – main idea of each paragraph
>   Green – important terms or names
>   Pink   – conclusions drawn by the author, etc.

BEFORE YOU BEGIN YOUR <u>ACTIVE READING</u>:

1.   Read over the chapter's Chief Learning Outcome; Learning Objectives; Key Concepts; Major Terms and Names; Review Questions; and Application Activities in this Study Guide. Read over any questions that may appear at the end of the chapter in the textbook. Also, read the Chapter Summary on your C-D Rom.

2.   Keep the list of Key Concepts, Major Terms and Names from the chapter handy during your reading time. Make it your goal to get command of the "language" of the reading assignment.

3.   Write the chapter title and list all major and minor headings included in the chapter. This will be your Chapter Outline. A good way to do this is to list these headings on the left of your page and write your notes to the right (see the sample sheet at the end of these strategies).

4.   Based on the chapter title and headings, as well as the Learning Objectives for the chapter in this Study Guide, list several questions you wish to answer as you read through the material.

AS YOU READ

1.   After reading the first few paragraphs of the chapter, stop and write a two-sentence summary in your own words.

2.   Write definitions/explanations for the Key Concepts, Major Terms and Names as you read through the chapter. Note those for which you require more information or explanation in order to understand them.

3. For each section of the reading material (or if the reading for a section is lengthy, every few paragraphs), stop and write a brief explanation of your understanding of the material. You may paraphrase, reword, or restate, but try to use your own words. *It has been said that this is where true learning takes place!*

4. As you read, make a written record of any material that you would like to have clarified.

   Write specific questions. For example, in Chapter 1 Conflict of Interest is discussed. The question, "What does conflict of interest mean?" would be too general. A more specific question might be, "What information is needed to determine whether there is a conflict of interest when a specific ethical question is raised?" As in the above example of a specific question, try to indicate in your questions what you do understand.

AT THE END OF YOUR READING

1. Look back at the questions. Are you now able to answer some or even all of these questions because you have completed your "active reading" of the entire chapter?

2. Create your own questions for the reading material. What questions would you include in a quiz on this chapter?

Good luck as you actively read BUSINESS ETHICS APPLIED !

CLASS/STUDY TIME

DAYS/TIME	SUN	MON	TUE	WED	THU	FRI	SAT
8 - 9 AM							
9 - 10 AM							
10 - 11 AM							
11 - 12 PM							
12 - 1 PM							
1 - 2 PM							
2 - 3 PM							
3 - 4 PM							
4 - 5 PM							
5 - 6 PM							
6 - 7 PM							
7 - 8 PM							
8 - 9 PM							
9 - 10 PM							
10 - 11 PM							

It will help if you consciously plan your study time. In college it is not unusual to allow two hours of study time for each hour in class. Fill in your class and work time, then plan enough ,study time for each class. Make an appointment with yourself and keep it. This will cut down on your stress level. Prepare daily, consider forming a study group, and read the text.

Try to schedule in some time for yourself and for your family and friends. In today's busy world it is difficult, but you will get more accomplished if you have a plan and work your plan.

APPLIED ETHICS

Be sure to take detailed notes. Try listing the key points to one side of your paper and on the right paraphase your lecture notes as well as those on the board. Then reread your notes and highlight the important items under each heading. You may wish to tape your key points and study by playing the tapes as you drive.

KEY POINTS/HEADINGS   **NOTES**

INTRODUCTION

 Chief Learning Outcome: I understand the symbolism and significance of the traffic light on the cover of the textbook.

 Learning Objectives

Given an opportunity to read and study this chapter, the student should be able to:

1. Describe what is meant by "a process of moral reasoning."
2. Summarize the author's definition of "situational ethics."
3. Explain what is symbolized by the "yellow light" and the significance of the traffic light.

 Major Terms and Names

(These may also appear in the questions below.)

1. process of moral reasoning
2. situational ethics
3. red light and green light
4. yellow light

Review Questions

Please write your answers directly in this Study Guide .

1. What does the author mean by the phrase "the process of moral reasoning"?

2. How does the author define "situational ethics"?

3. Explain what is symbolized by the "yellow light."

4. List the "five most important points" from your reading.
     a.

     b.

     c.

     d.

     e.
     1. – Compare your list with those of other students.
     2. – Compare, also, your textbook highlighting and margin notes.
     3. – Justify to each other what appears to be the major points and why.

☞ **Applications**

1. Consider the following ethical dilemma:
You have not had time to study for your first applied ethics exam, and the thought occurs to you that you could probably cheat on the exam without being caught.
     A. List four possible responses to this dilemma.
     B. Indicate how you would use **"red light, yellow light, green light"** to describe your possible choices.

2. In September of 1998, President Bill Clinton said: "I must always keep this as a caution light in my life." To what was he referring and what conflicts of interest confronted him in making decisions about that situation?

Is There a Universal Architecture?

In Chapter I we will observe four core values that seemed to be part of virtually any circumstance of critical thinking about moral problems. It is essential to be alert to what is happening around us, fair in the way we ask questions and organize information, caring in the decisions and actions we choose, and accountable in the way we resolve human problems. These four core values are also the very dimensions of personal moral growth that experts have tracked in the development of people from very early childhood to maturity. We will examine some of these experts' theories in Chapter II, gaining insight into moral development. In Chapter III we will disclose the role of logic in resolving human problems. Especially important will be knowledge of fallacies and the four steps of critical thinking:

Step One: Recognizing the problem.

Step Two: Engaging all available information.

Step Three: Making a decision and doing it.

Step Four: Explaining the decision.

These four steps of critical thinking make great use of *the four core values:*

Recognizing a problem takes **attentiveness**

Engaging all the valuable information takes **fairness**

Making a decision and doing it takes **care**

Explaining a decision takes **accountability**

Then in Chapters IV and V we will learn the dimensions of each of the classic and contemporary approaches to moral reasoning presented and how they tie into the four core values as well. Here is one way to say it:

Whatever our human **Substance** is, it enables our attentiveness.

Regardless of the **Principles**, we should apply them with fairness.

Because we use critical thinking, our **Actions** should show care.

Now that we own our ethics, we approach **Results** with accountability.

These four core values, then, are the basic human tools for understanding the ethics environment: be attentive, be fair, be caring, and be accountable.

VALUES

Arena	Self-directed	Other-directed
Personal values	n Becoming the kind of person I want to be n Being equipped for the kinds of achievements I want to make n Cultivating the right kinds of expectations from others	♦ Discerning moral character in others ♦ Being slow to judge others ♦ Learning skills of nurturing moral development in others
Friendship values	n Being the kind of person others will want to befriend n Becoming able to shape friendships for positive purposes n Having the moral fiber to be a faithful friend in difficult circumstances	♦ Discerning the difference between good and bad peer pressure ♦ Setting the "agenda" to protect relationships from abuse, and focus on good ♦ Understanding strengths and limits in friendships
Family values	n Honoring parents in appropriate ways n Having good relations with sisters/brothers n Being responsible in family relations	♦ Keeping the bonds strong in good times and bad ♦ Contributing to the good reputation of the family ♦ Avoiding traps of family patterns
Sexual values	n Becoming a self-disciplined woman or man n Differentiating between attraction and seduction n Committing to a life of faithfulness	♦ Understand the motives and drives of others ♦ Shaping and clarifying others' expectations ♦ Nurturing faithfulness in others
Consumer values	n Budgeting and using financial resources well n Reducing consumption of depletable resources n Acquiring responsible knowledge of product safety ecology, etc	♦ Supporting enterprises that benefit the community ♦ Encouraging ecologically wise policies ♦ Informing retailers and others of ethical concerns
Racial values	n Respecting your own race and its heritage n Learning about the harms of the past and being able to apologize and forgive n Developing ways of expressing sincere care	♦ Respecting others' races and racial heritage ♦ Detecting and addressing racial discrimination ♦ Coping positively with the sensitivies and felling of others
Employment values	n Learning good work ethics and work habits n Helping to shape a humane work environment n Being responsible and trustworthy	♦ Selecting a trustworthy and ethical employer ♦ Discerning co-workers' positive and negative motives ♦ Detecting and resolving human problems

Chapter I

ETHICS AND HUMAN CONFLICT

 Chief Learning Outcome: I can recognize moral issues and understand the role of ethics in solving human conflicts.

 Learning Objectives

Given an opportunity to read and study this chapter, the student should be able to:

1. Explain the meaning of all Key Concepts and the Major Terms and Names from the chapter and describe their relevance to the study of applied ethics.
2. Be able to define the three characteristics of this new way of thinking.
3. Recall the author's conclusion that "ethics is larger than the law."
4. Be able to distinguish between moral, nonmoral, immoral and amoral behavior.
5. Understand what "appearances are as important as reality" means.
6. Describe how disclosure can be an antidote to conflict of interest.

KEY CONCEPTS

Ethics is a discipline related to what is good and bad including moral duty and obligation, values and beliefs used in critical thinking about human problems.

Applied ethics is the actual use of moral standards of behavior in making decisions about human problems.

Business Ethics are standards related to what is good and bad including moral duty and obligation, values and beliefs used in critical thinking about behavior in the marketmlace.

Critical thinking is informed, reasoned and responsible human thought about human problems.

Conflict of interest is the predicament arising when a person confronts two actions that cannot be ethically reconciled; competing loyalties and concerns with others, self-dealing, outside compensation; divided loyalties among, for example, public and-or professional duties and private and-or personal affairs.

Moral means capable of distinguishing right from wrong with a predilection for right; as an adjective, it describes a person or act or thing that conforms to agreed-upon standards of conduct; as a noun, it is a summation of truth from an incident or parable.

Major Terms and Names

1. attentiveness
2. fairness
3. care
4. accountability
5. Judaism
6. Hinduism
7. Confucianism
8. Taoism
9. pluralistic society
10. protoplasm
11. perversity
12. disclosure

Review Questions

1. What are the three characteristics of this new way of "thinking about human problems"?

   a.

   b.

   c.

2. Define the following:

   • Moral

   • Nonmoral

   • Immoral

   • Amoral

3.   What is the meaning of the statement, "Ethics is larger than the law"?

4.   What is the meaning of the statement, "Appearances are as important as reality"?

5.   Describe how disclosure can be an antidote to conflict of interest.

6.   List the "five most important points" from your reading.

   a.

   b.

   c.

   d.

   e.

1.– Compare your list with those of other students.

2.– Compare, also, your textbook highlighting and margin notes.

3.– Justify to each other what appear to be the major points.

Applications

1.   Find two examples from the newspaper or a current news magazine of an actual or potential business or professional conflict of interest. Be sure that one article covers a political figure or governmental agency. Answer the following:

   a. What did this person/agency do and why is this a conflict or a potential conflict of interest?

   b. Would this conflict be easy or difficult to solve?

   c. How would you handle this conflict of interest if you were the person involved?

 **Cases**

PAPER JUSTICE - PART I

Click.

The nearly silent turnstile of the college library registered one more body. Kyle, a little bemused, glanced back at the "No Exit" sign now immediately behind him. The exit was a few feet away, next to the book check-out counter. It's good to know where the exit is, he thought with a chuckle.

Well, in Kyle's experience of two semesters, the library was not one of the more familiar parts of the college. He had been here a few times before, but only for a quiet place to study, or rest. This time he had to find a book, or even a few books. Kyle's research paper for ethics class was due the next Friday. It was certainly time to get started.

"Hey, hunk, you're right on time," Tricia whispered. She was in the same class. Tricia had agreed to help him use the computerized book search. "These computers will find what you're looking for in a minute. So, what topic did you choose for your paper"?

Kyle stroked his chin. "That's my first problem. You know I can do pretty well memorizing class notes for the tests, but this research stuff is something else. It's so new. My high school didn't prepare me for this at all. Would you believe, I've never written a research paper in my life."

"Oh, it's not so hard, Kyle," Tricia teased as she nudged her hand against his biceps. "I've written dozens of them."

"SSHHH!" Kyle warned firmly, and then started whispering again. "This is the library, Trish. I only told you one of my problems. Even if I knew how to do it, I really don't have any time. Chemistry reports, a project for management class, a big test in accounting - and I have to wait on tables at the restaurant every night. It's too much."

For several seconds they both silently stared at the blank computer screen in front of them.

"I have an idea," Tricia broke the silence with a very low voice, causing Kyle to lean a little closer to hear her better. "I have found so much material for my research I could easily write two papers. Really. Writing is such a breeze anyway. Then, when the restaurant closes Thursday night you can come over, look at what I've written for you, we could make some changes on my computer, and - *voila!* - your paper will be done. It's no problem." She grabbed his arm in a reassuring gesture.

1. Is there a problem here?
2. Does Kyle know what he is doing? Does Tricia know what she is doing?
   Is either one really alert to the real and potential problems involved?
3. Could Kyle have avoided his present crisis? Explain.

PAPER JUSTICE - PART II

"Tricia, you're too nice." Kyle was calling several hours later. Tricia had written down her phone number for him. "You are so sweet to offer to help. Frankly, I was getting depressed about all this work. You cannot imagine. Tricia, you're saving my life. But what can I do for you"?

"Don't worry about it, hunk. Something will come up. Maybe my car will break down again."

"How about chemistry? I'm getting mostly 'A's' there. I could show you my lab reports. It would definitely make your reports easier."

"Thanks but no thanks," Tricia said cautiously. "I'd rather struggle through it myself. If I'm going to make it in nursing, I'd better start thinking like a chemist now or I'll be really lost later on. But my car has some kind of terminal disease. Maybe you could come over and look at it Saturday when all your other work is out of the way. That's what I need."

Kyle didn't respond right away. After 10 seconds of silence, he started talking again slowly: "Hmmm. You know you're right. I wasn't thinking before. Now I don't know what to do."

"What do you mean? What's the problem?" Tricia was confused.

"You don't want me to help you with chemistry because you need to learn it. That makes sense. Shouldn't I do my own ethics paper for the same reason? I have to learn how to write a paper sometime. And, actually, Prof. Wier said each one of us should do our own research and writing. I'd better think about this again."

"Don't be silly, Kyle." Tricia was confident. "It's not at all like chemistry. Get real. You're not going to have to do ethics again once this course is out of the way, but chemistry is part of the lifeblood of my nursing career. I have to know what I'm doing there."

1. Is ethics at all like chemistry or not? Will "ethics" come up again in Tricia's and Kyle's lives? How?
2. Will Kyle face an ethical problem of cheating when he gets in business? Will Tricia face an ethical problem of cheating in nursing? How will they decide then? Will it make a difference to anyone?
3. What have you learned in ethics class - and in this chapter - that Kyle and Tricia seem to be forgetting?

PAPER JUSTICE - PART III

It was 11:30 Thursday night. For the past 20 minutes Kyle had, for the first time, been reading "his" research paper that Tricia had written for him for ethics class: "A Comparison of Plato and Rawls on the Standard of Justice in Society." It was kind of interesting; the style was smooth; it was long enough; and there were five books in the bibliography. Kyle made six or seven minor changes to make the paper fit more his own personal style, and ran it out of Tricia's printer.

"What a nice girl," he thought to himself, though he knew that "girl" is not quite the right word to use. How glad he was that they had talked after class a few days ago. There was no way he could have done a paper like this in the time he had. His life was so busy. Now he had a great paper to turn in.

Kyle half hugged Tricia while they both watched the printer finish the last page. "You're Wonder Woman. Let's take a look at your dying car this Saturday after lunch. I have to work the tables Saturday evening."

1. If he hands this paper in to Prof. Weir at the ethics class on Friday, what would, if anything, this say about Kyle's priorities?
2. What would it take for Kyle to change his mind about turning in this paper Tricia wrote? Could he ask Prof. Weir for an extension, and next week turn in something he would actually write himself?
3. Does Kyle respect Tricia? Does Tricia respect Kyle? What concept do they have of each other? How do they view themselves?

PAPER JUSTICE - PART IV

There it was again: "A Comparison of Plato and Rawls on the Standard of Justice in Society." Kyle silently re-read the title. Prof. Weir had just handed it back to him.

He quickly flipped past all of Tricia's work and the good professor's remarks. There on the last page was a "B+." Hmmm, not bad considering the amount of work I put into it," he mused to himself.

However, something else immediately caught his eye. Next to the "B+" Prof. Weir had attached a short note: "Kyle, this is a creative paper - good research and thoughtful comparisons. Nice job. I have a question for you about one of your points. If we can clarify it, your grade might go up, but we should talk about your ideas in any case. Please make an appointment soon."

1. Should Kyle make an appointment with Prof. Weir? Could he bluff knowledge of the subject of "his" paper? Should he try to bluff it?
2. Is Prof. Weir suspicious about whether Kyle really wrote the paper? What clues might he be going on?
3. What might Prof. Weir do if Kyle does not make the appointment to talk with him?

Chapter II

DIMENSIONS OF MORAL DEVELOPMENT

Chief Learning Outcome: I understand the stages of human moral development as theorized primarily by Kohlberg and Gilligan.

 Learning Objectives

Given an opportunity to read and study this chapter, the student should be able to:

1. Explain the meaning of all Key Concepts and the Major Terms and Names from the chapter and describe their relevance to the study of applied ethics.
2. Name two examples of historical figures who, through a sort of "moral conversion," were able to recognize a significant moral problem.
3. Name two examples of historical "heroes" who were perceptive of some major problems but "morally blind" to others.
4. Name Lawrence Kohlberg's three levels of moral development.
5. Recall the primary guidelines for each of Kohlberg's six stages of moral development.
6. Illustrate the roles of "behavior" vs. "motives" in determining Kohlberg's stages of moral development.
7. Outline the various "forms" the *Golden Rule* might "take" for each of Kohlberg's six stages of moral development.
8. Recognize a likely response to the *Heinz Dilemma* hypothetical representative of each of Kohlberg's six stages of moral development.
9. Derive two impressions from the reading of the selection from Kohlberg's *Education for Justice: A Modern Statement of the Socratic View* that aid in the understanding of Kohlberg's theory of moral development.
10. Recognize four contrasts among the "ways men and women tend to think" from Gilligan's *In A Different Voice* (excerpt).
11. Name four examples of historical figures who demonstrate what the author calls "real compatibility of reasoning and relationships."
12. Describe Gilligan's three steps of care.
13. Describe James Rest's ranking of women in Kohlburg's steps.
14. Outline Soren Kierkegaard's "three stages of life."
15. Name the seven steps of progression on Donald Osgood's "curve" representative of our development toward commitment.

KEY CONCEPTS

Moral development is human growth in the awareness of rightness and wrongness of actions, often accompanying physical maturity but not necessarily.

Kohlberg's six stages of moral development are Stage 1, Obedience/Punishment; Stage 2, Instrument and Relativity; Stage 3, Interpersonal Concordance; Stage 4, Law and Social Order; Stage 5, Social Contract; Stage 6, Universal Ethical Principles.

Gilligan's steps of moral development are (1) Care for self, (2) Care for others, (3) Balancing and Integrating self-interest and interests of others.

Kierkegaard's stages of life are (1) Aesthetic, (2) Ethical, (3) Religious.

Osgood's attitudes are (1) Idealistic, (2) Frustrated, (3) Defiant, (4) Resigned, (5) Aware, (6) Decisive, (7) Committed.

 ## Major Terms and Names

(These may also appear in the questions below.)

1. mixed motives
2. stages of awareness development
3. stages of justice
4. Lawrence Kohlberg
5. Kohlberg's levels and stages
6. justice
7. care
8. the Golden Rule
9. Carol Gilligan
10. Gilligan's steps
11. accountability
12. Soren Kierkegaard
13. Kierkegaard's stages of life
14. James Rest
15. Donald Osgood
16. Osgood's Attitude Curve

? Review Questions

1. Name two examples of historical figures who, through a sort of "moral conversion," were able to recognize a significant moral problem.
   a.

   b.

2. Two examples of historical "heroes" who were perceptive of some major problems but "morally blind" to others are:
   a

   b.

3. The three levels of Lawrence Kohlberg's Theory of Moral Development are:
   a.

   b.

   c.

4. The primary guidelines for each of Kohlberg's six stages of moral development are:
   Stage 1:

   Stage 2:

   Stage 3:

   Stage 4:

   Stage 5:

   Stage 6:

5. What are the roles of "behavior" vs. "motives" in determining Kohlberg's stages of moral development?

6. Outline the various "forms" the *Golden Rule* might "take" for each of Kohlberg's six stages of moral development.
Stage 1:

Stage 2:

Stage 3:

Stage 4:

Stage 5:

Stage 6:

7. For each of Kohlberg's six stages of moral development, give a likely response (as shared by the author) to the *Heinz Dilemma* hypothetical.
Stage 1:

Stage 2:

Stage 3:

Stage 4:

Stage 5:

Stage 6:

8. Read the selection from Kohlberg's *Education for Justice: A Modern Statement of the Socratic View.* What are two impressions gained from your reading of this selection that aid in your understanding of Kohlberg's Theory of Moral Development.

      a.

      b.

9. Four contrasts among the "ways men and women tend to think," according to Gilligan's *In a Different Voice* (excerpt), are:

      a.

      b.

      c.

      d.

10. Four examples of historical figures who demonstrate what the author calls "real compatibility of reasoning and relationships" are:

      a.

      b.

      c.

      d.

11. Describe Gilligan's "three steps of care."

      a.

      b.

      c.

12. Outline Soren Kierkegaard's "three stages of life."

      a.

      b.

      c.

13. According to James Rest, where do women rank in Kohlburg's steps?

14.   The seven steps of progression on Donald Osgood's "curve" representative of our development toward commitment are:

a.

b.

c.

d.

e.

f.

g.

15.   List the "five most important points" from your reading.

a.

b.

c.

d.

e.

1.– Compare your list with those of other students.

2.– Compare, also, your textbook highlighting and margin notes.

3.– Justify to each other what appear to be the major points.

Applications

1.   For each of Lawrence Kohlberg's six "stages of moral development," give an example of an instance when you or someone you have observed appears to have acted in accordance with that stage. For each example, explain why and how the behavior/motives illustrated appear to reflect that stage of development.

2.   For each of Carol Gilligan's three "steps of care," give an example of an instance when you or someone you have observed appears to have acted in accordance with that step. For each example, explain why and how the behavior/motives illustrated appear to reflect that step of care.

3.   For each of Soren Kierkegaard's three "stages of life," give an example of an instance when you or someone you have observed appears to have acted in accordance with that stage. For each example, explain why and how the behavior/motives illustrated appear to reflect that stage of life.

4.   For each of the "seven steps of progression" on Donald Osgood's curve, give an example of an instance when you or someone you have observed appears to have acted in accordance with that step. For each example, explain why and how the behavior/motives illustrated appear to reflect that step.

 Cases

Case 1: Consider the following hypothetical situation: Marie is newly graduated from college and has just been hired for a middle management position at an electronics company. Marie's boss, Tim, is one of the company's vice presidents; he also happens to be running for the office of County Commissioner. Marie has been given a company handbook that includes a provision expressly prohibiting the use of company time for any personal endeavors, including any work or activities associated with political campaigns. Tim has said to Marie, "That handbook doesn't really matter anyway," and has made it very clear that he expects Marie to help with his campaign (by making telephone calls, writing letters, etc.) during company time.

      A. What might be Marie's response at Stage 1 of Kohlberg's Theory? Stage 2? Stage 3? Stage 4? Stage 5? Stage 6?

      B. For each of the "responses" that you provide, also explain why and how the response is illustrative of that particular stage.

Chapter III

CRITICAL THINKING

 Chief Learning Outcome: I can apply critical thinking skills in making ethical arguments that avoid fallacious reasoning.

 Learning Objectives

Given an opportunity to read and study this chapter, the student should be able to:

1. Explain the meaning of all Key Concepts and the Major Terms and Names from the chapter and describe their relevance to the study of applied ethics.
2. Recall the meaning of critical thinking.
3. Recall why logic is useful as it relates to the application of ethics.
4. List the four steps of critical thinking.
5. List three steps involved in "engaging all the information" about a problem.
6. Recall five ways exemplars help in making ethical decisions.
7. Name the three parts of an argument.
8. Recall four general rules for argument structure.
9. Define deductive and inductive arguments, and give an original example of each.
10. Distinguish between valid and invalid arguments.
11. Explain how an argument is sound or unsound, cogent or uncogent.
12. Know the central distinctions among inductive arguments.
13. Describe the structure of a deductive argument.
14. Understand the meaning of fallacious reasoning.
15. Define the listed fallacies and give an original example of each type.
16. Understand the purpose of rejoinders.
17. Be able to apply ethical rationale.

KEY CONCEPTS

Critical Thinking Steps include recognizing a problem, engaging all available information, deciding what to do and doing it, being able to explain the decision to yourself and others. It makes use of arguments, reasoning and rationale.

Types of Arguments include deductive, inductive, valid and invalid, sound and unsound, cogent and uncogent.

Fallacious <u>reasoning</u> is an attempt to persuade emotionally or psychologically, not rationally, and involves statements that in one way or another deceive or mislead.

Ethical <u>rationale</u> correlates an argument with the standards of consistency, reasons, accountability, law, rules and the benefits of moral choices.

 ## <u>Major Terms and Names</u>

(These may also appear in the questions below.)

1. critical thinking
2. logic
3. human problems
4. exemplars
5. agreement
6. impartiality
7. integration
8. personal judgment
9. flexibility
10. grounds
11. structure
12. conclusion
13. inductive
14. deductive
15. valid
16. invalid
17. sound
18. unsound
19. cogent
20. uncogent
21. syllogism
22. general moral principle
23. informal fallacy
24. ambiguity
25. equivocation
26. amphiboly
27. genetic fallacy
28. *ad hominem* abusive
29. *ad hominem* circumstantial
30. faulty causation
31. *post hoc*
32. slippery slope
33. causal inference from a statistical correlation
34. false appeal to authority
35. argument to the people
36. invincible ignorance
37. argument from ignorance
38. inconsistency
39. straw man

40. red herring
41. either-or
42. hasty conclusion
43. two wrongs make a right
44. provincialism
45. is/ought confusion
46. questionable claim
47. rejoinders
48. consistency
49. reasons why
50. accountability
51. legal concerns
52. rules
53. benefits of moral choices

 Review Questions

1. What is critical thinking?

2. Why is logic helpful in the application of ethics ethics?

3. Name and explain the four steps of critical thinking.
   a.

   b.

   c.

   d.

4. What are the three sources involved in engaging all the information about a problem?
   a.

   b.

   c.

5.   What are five ways that approaches to moral reasoning help us in this new way of "thinking about human problems"?

a.

b.

c.

d.

e.

6   Name the three parts of an argument.

a.

b.

c.

7.   Name four general principles of argument structure as set forth by the author.

a.

b.

c.

d.

8.   Define the following, and give an original example of each.
deductive argument

inductive argument

9.   What are the distinguishing features of valid and invalid arguments?

10. What are the distinguishing features of sound and unsound arguments?

11. What are the distinguishing features of cogent and uncogent arguments?

12. Name and explain the two central distinctions among inductive arguments.

13. Describe the structure of a deductive moral argument.

14. What is meant by fallacious reasoning?

15. For the following fallacies, first define and then, where appropriate, give an original example.

a. ambiguity

equivocation

• example

amphiboly

- example

b. genetic fallacy

ad hominem abusive

- example

ad hominem circumstantial

- example

c. faulty causation

post hoc

- example

slippery slope

- example

statistical conclusion

- example

d. false appeal to authority

- example

e. argument to the people

- example

f. invincible ignorance

- example

g. ignorance

- example

h. inconsistency

- example

i. straw man

  • example

j. red herring

  • example

k. either–or

  • example

l. hasty conclusion

  • example

m. two wrongs make a right

  • example

n. provincialism

  • example

o. is-ought confusion

• example

p. questionable claim

• example

16.   What is the purpose of a rejoinder and what uses may be made of it?

17.   Discuss each of the six major standards required for the development of the ethical rationale necessary for justifying an ethical decision.

    a.

    b.

    c.

    d.

    e.

    f.

18.   List the "five most important points" from your reading.

a.

b.

c.

d.

e.

1.– Compare your list with those of other students.

2.– Compare, also, your textbook highlighting and margin notes.

3.– Justify to each other what appear to be the major points.

Applications

1.   Write a story illustrating a business situation. There should be at least four characters in your story, with dialogue for each. In the dialogue, include different examples of fallacious reasoning. (Note: It will be easier to do this if your story contains at least one moral dilemma.) At the end of the story, list the characters and explain how each character's reasoning is fallacious.

2.   For each of the following syllogisms, supply the missing premise(s) or conclusion:

a.
• It is immoral to accept illegal payment for professional services.
• A bribe is an illegal payment.
• _____

b.
• It is never morally right to break the law.
• _____
• Therefore, taking a bribe is morally wrong.

c.
• We have a moral obligation to feed those who are in poverty and are hungry.
•
_____

• Therefore, we have a moral obligation to provide food to Bosnia.

d.
•
_____
•
_____
• Therefore, it is morally wrong for students to bring machine guns on campus.

3.   Read and study Dr. Martin Luther King's letter that appears in the appendix, and answer the following questions:

    a. What is the purpose of Dr. King's letter? What prompted him to write it?
    b. Describe at least two of Dr. King's arguments in general terms.
    c. Write at least two syllogisms derived from Dr. King's arguments.

4.   Study the following syllogisms. Which are valid? Invalid? Explain your answers.

a.
• All grouper are fish.
• No mackerel is a grouper.
• Therefore, no mackerel is a fish.

b.
• No apples are citrus.
• Some fruit are apples.
• Therefore, some fruit is not citrus.

c.
• All ethics instructors are intelligent people.
• All intelligent people have master's degrees.
• Therefore, all ethics instructors have master's degrees.

5. Draw a picture of a syllogism. Label its parts with symbols other than those used in the chapter. Be creative! Share the picture with the class and explain how it illustrates a syllogism.

 Cases

Case. 1 Several weeks ago you promised your elderly aunt, who has always loved the circus, that you would take her to the Sunday afternoon performance when the circus came to town. It's late on Saturday evening; tomorrow afternoon's performance is the *last* and your aunt is planning to attend with you as you promised. Unfortunately, you have just realized that you have several assignments and projects due at work on Monday morning. As usual, you have procrastinated on getting those jobs done, yet you know your aunt is looking forward to her "circus date" with you. You cannot do both.

Use the four steps in critical thinking to address the case and to find a solution:
A.   What should you do?
B.   Be sure to show each of the steps and how they might be applied to this dilemma to reach a conclusion and find a solution.

Chapter IV

CLASSICAL APPROACHES TO MORAL REASONING

 Chief Learning Outcome: I am familiar with the five classical approaches to moral reasoning and I am developing my own particular worldview as a result.

Learning Objectives

Given an opportunity to read and study this chapter, the student should be able to:

1. Explain the meaning of all Key Concepts and the Major Terms and Names from the chapter and describe their relevance to the study of applied ethics.
2. Define an approach to moral reasoning.
3. Compare an ethical theory to a scientific theory.
4. Summarize the author's explanation of each approach to moral reasoning.
5. Explain the position/contribution of selected outstanding persons as they relate to one particular approach to moral reasoning.
6. Describe the focus and blind spots of each approach.
7. Discuss the strengths and weaknesses of each approach.
8. Recall the four sources which may be used to determine the will of God.
9. Recall the four virtues each of Plato and of Aristotle.
10. Discuss Aristotle's "eudaimonia" and his "golden mean."
11. Recall the fundamental natural law proclaimed by St. Thomas Aquinas.
12. Summarize communitarianism.
13. Recall the two concepts on which Kant based his theory.
14. Recall Kant's meaning of autonomy.
15. Discuss Kant's categorical imperative and its corollary.
16. Discuss *prima facie* obligations.

KEY CONCEPTS

The <u>Egoism</u> **Approach** emphasizes the aim of always acting for perceived self-interest, usually in the long term, even at the expense of the well-being of others.

The <u>Divine Command</u> **Approach** emphasizes that conduct is based on what is understood to be the will of God.

The **Virtue-Ethics** Approach emphasizes the aim of excellence by doing the right thing as a result of focusing on certain character values.

The **Natural Law** Approach emphasizes conduct based upon the perceived order inherent in the universe.

The **Deontology** Approach emphasizes basing conduct on a self-determined, innate sense of moral duty, with no regard for consequences.

 Major Terms and Names

(These may also appear in the questions below.)

1.   approach to moral reasoning
2.   SPAR dimensions
3.   Nietzsche
4.   Epicurus
5.   Thrasymachus
6.   Thomas Hobbes
7.   Adam Smith
8.   will of God
9.   H.L. Mencken
10. Moses
11. the Silver Rule
12. Socrates
13. the great awakenings
14. Abraham
15. Kierkegaard
16. Plato
17. Aristotle
18. eudaimonia
19. Nicomachean Ethics
20. "good"
21. moral virtues
22. intellectual virtues
23. golden mean
24. Stoics
25. Benjamin Franklin
26. Franklin's primary virtues
27. Johnson and Johnson's Credo
28. Pythagoras
29. St. Thomas Aquinas
30. C.S. Lewis
31. communitarianism
32. Dr. Martin Luther King Jr.
33. Confucius
34. Kant
35. duty
36. goodwill
37. autonomy

38. Categorical Imperative
39. maxim
40. respect for persons
41. Sartre
42. William David Ross
43. prima facie obligations
44. Christianity
45. individualism
46. Islam
47. Judaism

 **Review Questions**

1.   Define an approach to moral reasoning (ethical theory).

2.   Explain how an ethical theory will function like a scientific theory.

3.   Summarize the author's explanation of the egoism approach to moral reasoning.

4.   Explain the position/contributions of Hobbes, Smith and Nietzsche as they relate to the egoistic approach.

5.   Describe the focus and blind spots of the egoism approach.

6.   Discuss the strengths and weaknesses of egoism.

7.   Summarize the author's explanation of the divine command approach.

8.   Name the four sources from which the divine command follower may determine the will of God.
       a.

       b.

       c.

       d.

9.   Explain the position and contributions of Moses, Abraham, and Kierkegaard as they relate to the divine command approach.

10.   Discuss the focus and blind spots of the divine command approach.

11.   Discuss the strengths and weaknesses of the divine command approach.

12.   Summarize the author's explanation of the virtue-ethics approach to moral reasoning.

13.   What were Plato's four classical virtues?
       a.
       b.
       c.
       d.

14.   What did Aristotle mean by eudaimonia?

15.   Define the central feature of Aristotle's view.

16.   What were the four virtues emphasized by Aristotle.
       a.
       b.
       c.
       d.

17.   Explain the position/contributions of Plato, Aristotle and Benjamin Franklin as they relate to the virtue approach.

18. Discuss the focus and blind spots of the virtue ethics approach.

19. Discuss the strengths and weaknesses of virtue ethics.

20. Summarize the author's explanation of the natural law approach.

21. What was the fundamental natural law proclaimed by St. Thomas Aquinas?

22. Define communitarianism.

23. Explain the position and contributions of St. Thomas Aquinas and Dr. Martin Luther King Jr. as they relate to the natural law approach?

24. Discuss the strengths and weaknesses of natural law.

25. Summarize the author's explanation of the deontological approach to moral reasoning.

26. Explain the position and contributions of Confucius, Kant and Sartre as they relate to the deontological approach.

27. On what two concepts did Kant base his ethical reasoning?
   a.

   b.

28. What did Kant mean by autonomy?

29. Define and discuss the Categorical Imperative and its corollary.

30. Discuss the focus and blind spots of the deontological approach.

31. Discuss the strengths and weaknesses of deontology.

32. What did Ross believe were *prima facie* obligations?

33.　　List the "five most important points" from your reading.

　　　　a.

　　　　b.

　　　　c.

　　　　d.

　　　　e.

　　　　1.– Compare your list with those of other students.

　　　　2.– Compare, also, your textbook highlighting and margin notes.

　　　　3.– Justify to each other what appear to be the major points.

Applications

1.　　Do you recognize some of the moral theories described in this chapter as ones you have been taught before? If so, which ones are they?

2.　　For each of the approaches described in the chapter, list the steps a person would be required to undertake in applying this particular approach to moral reasoning. As an example: The steps a person would undertake in applying the traditional divine-command approach to any moral dilemma might be listed as follows:

　　Step a. Identify the moral issue. What is the decision that needs to be made?

　　Step b. Consult various resources to determine what God's will would be in this particular situation, including sacred scriptures, prayer, conscience, and religious authorities.

　　Step c. Make a decision conforming behavior to what is determined to be God's will.

3.　　Prepare your own virtue chart based on the Franklin chart which follows, using at least four virtues of your interest, not necessarily any of Franklin's. Keep a record of your progress for four weeks. Then write a one-page paper discussing the experience.

Benjamin Franklin's Virtue Chart

Virtue	Sunday	Monday	Tuesday	Wednesday	Thursday	Friday	Saturday
Temperance							
Silence							
Order							
Resolution							
Frugality							
Industry							
Sincerity							
Justice							
Moderation							
Cleanliness							
Tranquillity							
Chastity							
Humility							

 **Cases**

Case 1. Greg has a lower level supervisory position with a major corporation, however he has an opportunity for a major promotion once he has earned his degree. (A degree is mandatory in the Managment Training Program.) His company will pay his college expenses as long as Greg earns a "C" or better.

Greg is facing his last college exam tonight; he has not had the opportunity to study adequately. He works more than 50 hours a week, he is married and has two small children, and the demands of family and job are almost more than he can handle.

Greg is in the library just hours before the exam. He notices some of the other students from his class huddled around one of the tables and joins them; he discovers that they are talking to a young man who has somehow obtained a copy of the exam from the instructor's private files. It seems apparent that this could be an opportunity to do well on the test in spite of his lack of opportunity to study.

A. Choose one of the approaches to moral reasoning, and using the "steps" you outlined for that approach, resolve the dilemma in accordance with the theory. Be sure to use all of the steps and to show how they would apply in this particular dilemma.

B. If Greg chose to cheat and you, as his boss, were to later learn that he received his degree by cheating on his last exam-----what would your reaction be?

Chapter V

CONTEMPORARY APPROACHES TO MORAL REASONING

 Chief Learning Outcome: I am familiar with three contemporary approaches to moral reasoning and I am developing my own particular worldview as a result.

 Learning Objectives

Given an opportunity to read and study this chapter, the student should be able to:

1. Explain the meaning of all Key Concepts and the Major Terms and Names from the chapter and describe their relevance to the study of applied ethics.
2. Summarize the author's explanation of each approach to moral reasoning in this chapter.
3. Explain the position/contributions of selected outstanding persons as they relate to one particular approach to moral reasoning in the chapter.
4. Describe the focus and blind spots of each approach.
5. Discuss the difference between Act and Rule utility.
6. Recall Bentham's use of hedonistic calculus in utilitarianism.
7. Recall the contemporary utilitarian business concept influenced by Bentham and its application in the Ford Pinto case.
8. Recall and discuss Rawls's "veil of ignorance," and his principles of equal liberty, equal opportunity and the difference principle.
9. Recall two of the major contracts affecting America today.
10. Discuss the "cunning" of reason.

 KEY CONCEPTS

The **Consequentialist** Approach emphasizes conduct determined by assessing the moral quality of the *results* likely to follow from various possible courses of actions.

The **Utilitarian** Approach emphasizes always acting in order to produce the most amount of satisfaction (pleasure or happiness) and the least amount of dissatisfaction (pain or unhappiness) for the greatest number of people.

The **Contractarian** Approach emphasizes that all ethical obligation is based exclusively upon contracts and promises.

The **Natural Rights** Approach emphasizes the exclusive protection of and reliance upon common human personal rights.

 Major Terms and Names

(These may also appear in the questions below.)

1. consequentialism
2. principle of utility
3. Jeremy Bentham
4. hedonistic calculus
5. John Stuart Mill
6. Rule Utilitarianism
7. Act Utilitarianism
8. cost-benefit analysis
9. William James
10. the Pinto case
11. John Rawls
12. veil of ignorance
13. reflective equilibrium
14. equal liberty principle
15. equal opportunity principle
16. difference principle
17. respect of others
18. Thomas Jefferson
19. John Locke
20. Martin Luther King Jr.
21. Donald Dworkin
22. Declaration of Independence
23. United Nations Universal Declaration of Human Rights
24. cunning
25. George W.F. Hegel
26. integrated person

 Review Questions

1. Summarize the author's explanation for the consequentialist approach to moral reasoning.

2.   Summarize the author's explanation for the utilitarian approach to moral reasoning.

3.   Explain the position and contributions of Mill and Bentham as they relate to the utilitarian approach.

4.   Explain the difference between Act and Rule utility.

5.   Describe Bentham's hedonistic calculus method for reaching a moral decision.

6.   Define the contemporary business concept greatly influenced by Bentham.

7.   Discuss the focus and blind spots of the utilitarian approach.

8.   Discuss the utilitarian aspects of the Pinto case.

9.   Discuss the strengths and weaknesses of utilitarianism.

10.   Summarize the author's explanation for the contractarian approach.

11.   Define and discuss Rawls's "veil of ignorance."

12.   Discuss the focus and blind spots of the contractarian approach.

13.   Define the following:

equal liberty principle

equal opportunity principle

difference principle

14.   Discuss the strengths and weaknesses of contractarianism.

15.   Summarize the author's explanation for the natural rights approach.

16.   Explain the position and contributions of Locke, Martin Luther King Jr. and Dworkin as they relate to the natural rights approach.

17.   Discuss the focus and blind spots of the natural-rights approach.

18.   Name and discuss two major contracts that affect America today.

        a.

        b.

19.   Discuss the strengths and weaknesses of natural rights.

20.   Define the "cunning" of reason.

21. List the "five most important points" from your reading.

a.

b.

c.

d.

e.

1.– Compare your list with those of other students.

2.– Compare, also, your textbook highlighting and margin notes.

3.– Justify to each other what appear to be the major points.

Applications

1. Draft your own worldview in light of your review of all eight approaches to moral reasoning covered in Chapters 4 and 5. Using the chart that follows, note what aspect(s) of each approach may or may not be part of your own worldview.

2. For each of the approaches described in the chapter, list the steps a person would be required to undertake in applying this particular approach to moral reasoning. As an example: The steps a person would undertake in applying the traditional divine-command approach to any moral dilemma might be listed as follows:

Step a.   Identify the moral issue. What is the decision that needs to be made?

Step b.   Consult various resources to determine what God's will would be in this particular situation, including sacred scriptures, prayer, conscience, and religious authorities.

Step c.   Make a decision conforming behavior to what is determined to be God's will.

 ## Cases

Case 1. Greg has a lower level supervisory position with a major corporation, however he has an opportunity for a major promotion once he has earned his degree. (A degree is mandatory in the Managment Training Program.) His company will pay his college expenses as long as Greg earns a "C" or better.

Greg is facing his last college exam tonight; he has not had the opportunity to study adequately. He works more than 50 hours a week, he is married and has two small children, and the demands of family and job are almost more than he can handle.

Greg is in the library just hours before the exam. He notices some of the other students from his class huddled around one of the tables and joins them; he discovers that they are talking to a young man who has somehow obtained a copy of the exam from the instructor's private files. It seems apparent that this could be an opportunity to do well on the test in spite of his lack of opportunity to study.

A. Choose one of the approaches to moral reasoning, and using the "steps" you outlined for that approach, resolve the dilemma in accordance with the theory. Be sure to use all of the steps and to show how they would apply in this particular dilemma.

B. If Greg chose to cheat and you, as his boss, were to later learn that he received his degree by cheating on his last exam-----what would your reaction be?

THE BIG PICTURE
A Comparison of Approaches to Moral Reasoning

Approach, Or Theory	Concept of the Person	Principles that Matter	Actions that Fit the Model	Results that Are Sought
1. Egoism	Center of power; Exploiter.	Make your own decisions. Be authentic	Self-centered; Individuality or fear of punishment.	Personal authenticity and freedom.
2. Divine Command	Person endowed by the Creator with a purpose.	Fulfill the intentions and commands of the Creator.	Creator-centered: Obedience and honor for the Deity.	Positive relationship and peace with the Creator.
3. Virtue	Individual with developing habits and personality.	Cultivate behaviors that improve human flourishing.	Concordant with intended and helpful habits.	Healthy, balanced, and flourishing character.
4. Natural Law	Personality built-in needs, instincts, and goals.	Live harmoniously with your true essence.	Expressive of the natural qualities and needs.	Fulfillment of intrinsic patterns and potential.
5. Deontologism	Law-maker and law follower.	Follow (deductively) the imperatives that you accept.	Consistent with selected general imperatives.	A good will, one that acts according to chosen principles.
6. Consequentialism	Maximizer of good consequences, and minimizer of bad.	Produce the greatest happiness of the greatest number.	Prudent and mindful of probable good consequences.	Maximum benefit to the most people that are involved.
7. Contractarianism	Rational, reliable and reflective negotiator.	Develop rules and relationships that all can affirm.	conforming with agreed interests and rules.	Self-adjusting group of rational rule-followers.
8, Natural Rights	Somebody worthy of protection and respect.	Never harm the rights of any person involved.	Responsible, protective, and thoughtful.	Complete protection of every person involved.
9. Composite Example	Sensitive, informed, adaptable, creative, rational decision-maker	Select outstanding insights and blend them into coherent perspective and commitment.	Perceptive, just, loving, flexible, consistent, sagacious action.	Attentive, fair, caring responsible individuals and communities.
10. My World view				

INTEGRATED WORLDVIEW:

Dr. Martin Luther King, Jr.	
1. Egoism	"Any true alliance is based upon some self-interest of each component group and a common interest into which they merge. For alliance to have permanence and loyal commitment from its various elements, each of them must have a goal from which it benefits and none must have an outlook in basic conflict with the others" (T, 309)
2. Divine Command	"Dr. King probably never spoke or wrote without quoting the Bible. He also referred to God's authority rather often . . . "god is interested in the freedom of the whole human race and in the creation of a society where all men can live together as brothers, where every man will respect the dignity and the worth of human personality." (T, 215)
3. Virtues Ethics	"[The method of nonviolence] not only avoids external physical violence, but also internal violence of spirit. At the center of nonviolence stands the principle of love. In struggling for human dignity the oppressed people of the world must not succumb to the temptation of becoming bitter . . ." (T, 87)
4. Natural-Law	" . . . let us remember that there is a creative force in this universe, working to pull down the gigantic mountains of evil, a power that is able to make a way out of no way and transform dark yesterdays into bright tomorrow's. Let us realize the arc of the moral universe is long but it bends toward justice." (T, 252)
5. Deontologism	" . . . nonviolent resistance breaks with communism and with all those systems which argue that the end justifies the means, because we realize that the end is preexistent in the means. In the long run of history, destructive means cannot bring about constructive ends." (T, 214)
6. Consequentialism	"And when we allow freedom to ring . . . we will be able to speed up that day when all of God's children - black and white men, Jews and Gentiles, Catholics and Protestants - will be able to join hands and to sing in the words of the old Negro spiritual, 'Free at last, free at last; thank God Almighty, we are free at last.'" (T, 220)
7. Contractarianism	"So we've come here today to dramatize a shameful condition. In a sense we've come to our nation's capital to cash a check. When the architects of our republic wrote the magnificent words of the constitution and the Declaration of Independence, they were signing a promissory note to which every American was to fall heir." (Testament of Hope, p. 217)
8. Natural-Rights	[Continuing from the previous quotation . . .] "This note was the promise that all men, yes, black men as well as white men, would be guaranteed the unalienable rights of life, liberty, and the pursuit of happiness." (Testament of Hope, p. 217)
9. Composition Perspectives	" . . . nonviolent resistance . . . combines being tough-minded and tender-hearted and avoids the complacency and apathy of the soft minded and the violence and bitterness of the hard-hearted." (Strength to Love, p. 19)

INTEGRATED PERSON

John Marks Templeton	
1. Egoism	[Egoism comes out the weakest in Templeton's wisdom. However, for him it is essential to develop yourself. On this approach he approvingly quotes Coleman Cox - "I am a great believer in luck. The harder I work, the more of it I seem to have" - and Louis Pasteur - "Chance favors the prepared mind."] *(The Templeton Plan* (TTP), pp. 62, 63.)
2. Divine Command	"Simply pray often in the day: "Thy will be don." This simple prayer empties the mind of preconceptions, and makes it more open to God's wisdom." (TTP, p. 131.) "No one should expect that, just because he begins with prayer, every decision he makes is going to be profitable. However, I do believe that if you pray, you will make fewer stupid mistakes... Backed by our beliefs, we're not so uptight and on edge as those who are in the business merely to make money. We start each day by setting our minds on the important things and praying. All our transactions are influenced by that." (TTP, p. ix.)
3. Virtues Ethics	"All of us believe in virtue, but few of us give much thought to the varieties of virtue that exist and to their relative spiritual weights... No matter what career you might embark on, success comes from knowing the importance of virtues. It is not enough to live them unconsciously, you must struggle to *know* them and live them consciously." (TTP, pp. 23,24.)
4. Natural-Law	"That greed and callousness are shortsighted business methods is a crucial lesson for us all to absorb. Learning it will spell success. You should always care about your customer. You should treat your employee as you want to be treated. If you follow those precepts, which are rooted in religion, financial success is likely to follow." (TTP, p. v.)
5. Deontologism	"The way to capture happiness is to try to do something not directly aimed at giving you pleasure... Happiness and success are awarded to those who do not seek them as ends in themselves but struggle to excel at a given task... Happiness pursued eludes; happiness given returns." (TTP, pp. 28,2.) "Successful people finish what they begin. Be sure to think carefully before you take on a task, but, once you start it, complete it with thoroughness, energy, and resolve." (TTP, p.77.)
6. Consequentialism	Templeton explains that he writes to provide "a set of rules to help readers increase their quotient of happiness and prosperity... To overcome the problems we face - and no life is problem-free - it is crucial to have a plan to live by." (TTP, p. v.)
7. Contractarianism	"I am convinced that the basic principles for happiness and success can be examined, tested, and agreed upon." (TTP, p. vi.)
8. Natural-Rights	"[The Reformation as well as scientific discoveries helped produce the free world where] the individual is important, where a man's or woman's opinion should be listened to, where each person has a right to choose the basics of a decent life: career, marriage partner, school, religion, place of residence, and free speech... Freedom fosters competition which yields progress." *(The Humble Approach, p. 81.)*
9. Other Perspectives	"Humility is the gateway of knowledge. To learn more, we must first realize how little we already know. the unknown before us may be a million times greater than what we now know, despite the myriad discoveries made in recent years." *(The Humble Approach, p. 11.)*

Endnote 8

INTEGRATED PERSON:

You	
1. Egoism	
2. Divine Command	
3. Virtues Ethics	
4. Natural-Law	
5. Deontologism	
6. Consequentialism	
7. Contractarianism	
8. Natural-Rights	
9. Other Perspectives	

Chapter VI

ECONOMIC JUSTICE

Chief Learning Outcome: I understand the concept of economic justice and am able to discuss various moral theories as they apply to a nation's economy.

 Learning Objectives

Given an opportunity to read and study this chapter, the student should be able to:

1. Explain the meaning of all Key Concepts and the Major Terms and Names from the chapter and describe their relevance to the study of applied ethics.
2. Recall John Locke's assumption in his *Second Treatise On Government.*
3. List three definitions offered by Robert Nozick for the purpose of understanding the entitlement theory.
4. Summarize the two qualifications on the right to obtain property contained in the Lockean proviso.
5. Recognize the fundamental assumption of John Rawls' theory of justice, and recall the basic requirement and its two potential problems as he defines it.
6. Recite the guiding idea behind Rawls' conception of justice.
7. Recognize the reason for Rawls' "veil of ignorance."
8. Recall two assumptions about Rawls' "original position."
9. Summarize two fundamental principles of justice that Rawls believes would be adopted by those in the original position behind the veil of ignorance.
10. Explain classical republicanism.
11. Define communitarianism.
12. Summarize the author's comparisons and contrasts of the three theories of distributive justice covered in the chapter.
13. Recall two major points from Adam Smith's argument against mercantilism.
14. Summarize three of the major points from Karl Marx's *Capital.*
15. Explain Marx's concern regarding the "inherent instability" associated with free-market capitalism.
16. Summarize some of the arguments *pro* and *con* of the two alternative economic systems.
17. Recall the principal advantage of a mixed economic system, as offered by the author.
18. Define three categories of tax, with respect to issues of distributive justice.
19. Recall two points in support of welfare as a "right" and two points in support of welfare as a "privilege."
20. Recall Thomas Malthus's conclusion in *Wealth of Nations.*
21. Recall how developmentalists respond to the neo-Malthusian emphasis on overpopulation as the primary cause of world hunger.
22. Summarize the Kantian/Shue point of view regarding moral requirements for responding to world hunger.

 **KEY CONCEPTS**

Retributive Justice is justice which fairly and appropriately punishes some prior wrongdoing.

Distributive Justice is justice which fairly and appropriately distributes everything from economic goods and services to public honors and awards.

Entitlement Theory is the theory of distributive justice seen in John Locke and characterized by Robert Nozick by three premises:
1) All people are entitled to that which they acquire justly.
2) All people are entitled to that which is justly transferred to them from someone else who justly acquired that which was transferred.
3) No person is entitled to anything except by (repeated) applications of (1) and (2).

Patterned Principle of Distribution is any principle of distribution of resources that holds out some pattern according to which the good should be allocated such as one in which all people have the same amount of good (egalitarianism) or in which the worst of people have as much as possible (sometimes called the *maximum* pattern because the person with the minimum has the maximum that he or she can have). Patterned principles of distribution are contrasted with principles such as those in entitlement in which no particular pattern is held out as the right one, but rather the right distribution is simply whatever arises from free acquisition and transfer.

Egalitarianism is the patterned theory of distribution in which the goal is to arrange resources so that people have equal amounts. Some principles may be relatively egalitarian, such as Rawls's difference principle, which justifies inequalities provided they serve to benefit the worst off, while others may be more radically egalitarian, rejecting even inequalities that benefit the worst off.

The Difference Principle is the principle of John Rawls stating that differences in the amount of primary social goods are justified provided the differences improve the position of the worst off compared to what they would have if there were more equality.

Classical Republicanism is the political philosophy having its roots in Aristotle and Thomas Aquinas that holds the human has an essential nature that includes rationality, sociability, and membership in the animal kingdom. This essential nature permits distinction between human needs and mere human wants. A just distribution of resources is one that uses resources to meet needs rather than desires.

Communitarianism is the view of contemporary philosophers who emphasize the importance of the human as a social being who is part of a community rather than primarily an isolated individual. Communitarians generally favor the Classical Republican theory of justice and communal decisions about the use of resources rather than leaving such choices up to the individual.

A "Thin" Conception of the Good is a conception of what is good for which there is agreement on only the most primary or general and abstract goods such as liberty, political and economic opportunities, secure and adequate income, wealth, and self-respect. These are goods that any person would desire no matter what his or her more specific desires. This view is generally held by liberals, both Entitlement theorists and egalitarians. It contrasts with the "thick" conception of the good usually held by Classical Republicans and communitarians.

Capitalism is an economic system where all property (including factories and other "means of production") is privately owned and operated for individual profit as determined by a free market.

Socialism is an economic system in which all the means of production are socially owned and operated for the good of the public as a whole.

Mixed Economic System is an economic system in which some of the means of production are privately owned while others are publicly owned.

 Major Terms and Names

(These may also appear in the questions below.)

1. John Locke
2. Robert Nozick
3. acquire justly
4. justly transfer
5. Lockean proviso
6. John Rawls
7. burdens and benefits
8. social contract theories
9. veil of ignorance
10. "justice as fairness"
11. rational
12. primary good
13. liberty
14. difference principle
15. theory of human nature
16. liberal theory of justice
17. moral freedom
18. right desire
19. just distribution of goods
20. modern liberalism
21. mercantilism
22. Karl Marx
23. surplus value
24. taxation
25. standards for determining income
26. inequality
27. three kinds of taxes
28. disparate results
29. welfare
30. Thomas Malthus
31. neo-Malthusian
32. Garrett Hardin
33. developmentalist
34. Peter Singer
35. Henry Shue

❓ Review Questions

1. What is the assumption upon which John Locke's *Second Treatise On Government* is based?

2. Three definitions offered by Robert Nozick for the purpose of understanding the entitlement theory are:
    a.

    b.

    c.

3. Summarize the two qualifications on the right to obtain property contained in the Lockean proviso.
    a.

    b.

4. What is the fundamental assumption of John Rawls's theory of justice, and what is the basic requirement and its two potential problems, as he defines it?

5. What is the guiding idea behind Rawls's conception of justice?

6. What is the reason for Rawls' "veil of ignorance"?

7.   List two assumptions about Rawls's original position.
        a.

        b.

8.   Summarize the two fundamental principles of justice that Rawls believes
would be adopted by those in the original position behind the veil of ignorance.
        a.

        b.

9.   Explain classical republicanism.

10. Define communitarianism.

11. Three of the author's points about modern liberalism are:
        a.

        b.

        c.

12. Summarize the author's comparisons and contrasts of the three theories of
distributive justice covered in the chapter.

13. List two major points from Adam Smith's argument against mercantilism.
    a.

    b.

14. List three of the major points from Karl Marx's *Capital*.
    a.

    b.

    c.

15. Explain Marx's concern regarding the "inherent instability" associated with free-market capitalism.

16. Summarize the arguments pro and con of the two alternative economic systems defined by the author.

17. What, according to the author, is the principal advantage of a mixed system?

18. With respect to issues of distributive justice, three categories of taxation are:
    a.

    b.

    c.

19. Two points in support of welfare as a "right" and two points in support of welfare as a "privilege" are as follows:
    welfare as a "right"

    a.

    b.

    welfare as a "privilege"

    a.

    b.

20. What is Thomas Malthus's conclusion in *Wealth of Nations*?

21. How do developmentalists respond to the neo-Malthusian emphasis on overpopulation as the primary cause of world hunger?

22. Summarize the Kantian/Shue point of view regarding moral requirements for responding to world hunger.

23.   List the "five most important points" from your reading.
    a.

    b.

    c.

    d.

    e.

    1.– Compare your list with those of other students.

    2.– Compare, also, your textbook highlighting and margin notes.

    3.– Justify to each other what appear to be the major points.

Applications

1.   Do you think the media play a significant role in influencing our attitudes and views about economic justice? Explain your answer and include examples.

2.   What do you think is the prevailing view concerning world hunger among your peer group? Would you classify that predominant view as morally responsible? Why or why not?

3.   Do you believe America and other wealthy, developed nations have an ethical responsibility to help underdeveloped nations? Why or why not? If yes, what actions should we be taking to help? On what general ethical principles do you base your position?

4.   What do you think about the governmental programs currently in place in our country for alleviating poverty? Is our government doing enough for people? Is it doing too much? Are there any changes you would advocate? On what general ethical principles do you base your position?

5.   Recall Rawls's second fundamental principle, the "difference principle." Refer to the information in the textbook about this principle, including the sample table given. Create your own hypothetical scenario demonstrating the difference principle.

 **Cases**

Case 1. The year is 2003. India has been facing a significant famine for the past three years. This year a million Indians will die if the countries in the West don't offer significant contributions in food and foreign aid. It wasn't always like this. Prior to the drought, India was agriculturally self-sufficient. In fact, India was even able to export some grain. But it wasn't just the drought that caused India's troubles. For the past decade the cost of oil had been rising dramatically. This in turn led to a huge increase in the cost of nitrogen fertilizer. And then there was the most recent presidential election in the United States.

Three years ago the winning candidate ran on the platform of "putting Americans first" and holding down increasing fuel costs. One of her first acts as President was to ban the export of any petroleum-based products, including fertilizers. Prior to the drought, this didn't seem like a particularly controversial move. But now, many Americans have said her policies were responsible for the deaths of thousands.

Partly in response to demonstrations at home, and partly out of her own moral convictions, the President promised to increase American foreign aid from .2% to the .7% recommended by the United Nations - but only if the other "G-7" countries would do likewise. This began a series of long and drawn-out negotiations in Europe and Japan.

However, while members of the "G-7" were trading proposals, thousands of Indians were dying each day. India's Prime Minister was herself facing tremendous pressure to do something to save her people. During one of her sleepless nights she recalled the Thomistic principle she had learned while studying in England: "It is not theft, properly speaking, to take secretly and use another's property in cases of extreme need." Though she could hardly "take secretly" from the grain elevators of the "G-7," she did have at her control several nuclear weapons. Harkening back to a scenario that was discussed in the 1970s, she took action: She ordered her military leaders to ship four nuclear bombs in unmarked containers rigged with remote control detonators to major ports in four different countries. After they arrived, she made the following demand: "Either the G-7 negotiators come to an agreement in the next 12 hours, or I will order one bomb to be exploded for each day you delay."

Needless to say, the Prime Minister's plan is not without risks. There is no way she can prevent the threatened nations from launching their own pre-emptive strike, killing her and millions of other Indians. Of course, such a strike is itself extremely risky because it would do nothing to save the cities of the "G-7."

    a. Has the Prime Minister of India correctly applied Thomas's principle?
    b. Irrespective of the political wisdom of the Prime Minister's action, can it be justified *morally*?
    c. In a press conference after her announcement, the Prime Minister justifies her threat to kill millions of *individually* innocent people by arguing that because they had been the recipients of *corporate or national* economic advantages all their lives, it is only just that they share the corporate or national "burdens" as well. Is she correct?
    d. To bomb the cities of another nation is universally acknowledged to be an act of war. Is it an act of war for one nation to withhold essential exports for another nation's survival?

Additional Questions:
    a. List as many moral issues as you can surrounding the situation described.
    b. Apply one or more approaches to moral reasoning. Each time you apply an approach, be sure to include the following:
        1. What steps would be undertaken with that approach, and how would those steps apply specifically to the case?

2. Based on applying the steps and showing how they would "work" in this particular case, what might be the ultimate resolution?
3. Write at least one syllogism in response to the dilemma that the case presents. Make sure each syllogism reflects a general moral principle embodied in the approach/theory of moral reasoning you have applied.

Chapter VII

CODES OF ETHICS

 Chief Learning Outcome: I understand the role and development of codes of ethics in business, professions and government.

 Learning Objectives

Given an opportunity to read and study this chapter, the student should be able to:

1. Explain the meaning of all Key Concepts and the Major Terms and Names from the chapter and describe their relevance to the study of applied ethics.
2. Recall three points that would support the conclusion that codes of ethics are necessary.
3. Explain three ways in which codes of ethics may vary.
4. Name three findings of the Ethics Resource Center study on corporate codes of ethics.
5. List four reasons why a corporation might want to develop a code of ethics.
6. Name three kinds of behaviors often included in corporate codes of ethics.
7. Define "mixed message" and recall one example as it relates to corporate codes of ethics.
8. Restate the 10 principles listed in the chapter for quality codes of ethics.
9. Describe various levels of codes of ethics.
10. Summarize Robert E. Sweeney's five steps in the development of a corporate code of ethics.
11. Recall three ways in which professional codes of ethics are different from corporate codes.
12. Discuss DeGeorge's four characteristics of a viable professional code.
13. Name three potential limitations of professional codes.
14. Recall three processes by which a professional code of ethics can be evaluated.
15. Name three ways in which government and public service codes of ethics vary.
16. List three strengths and three weaknesses of government/public service codes.

KEY CONCEPTS

Codes of ethics are written sets of principles and rules intended to serve as a guideline for determining appropriate ethical behavior for those individuals under its authority.

Categories of codes include corporate, professional and government and public service.

Major Terms and Names

(These may also appear in the questions below.)

1. moral code
2. Richard DeGeorge
3. "loophole mentality"
4. William Shaw
5. authorship
6. ethical level
7. Johnson and Johnson's Credo
8. Cecily A. Raiborn and Dinah Payne
9. Ethics Resource Center, Washington, D.C.
10. corporate culture
11. mixed message
12. Robert E. Sweeney
13. Jacqueline Dunckel
14. Dunckel's six "lessons"
15. profession
16. revolving door lobbying
17. whistle-blowing

 Review Questions

1. List three points that would support the conclusion that codes of ethics are necessary.

   a.

   b.

   c.

2. List three ways in which codes may vary.

   a.

   b.

   c.

3. Identify the three findings of the Ethics Resource Center study on corporate codes of ethics.

     a.

     b.

     c.

4. Name four of the reasons why a corporation might want to develop a code of ethics.

     a.

     b.

     c.

     d.

5. Three kinds of behaviors often included in corporate codes of ethics are:

     a.

     b.

     c.

6. Define "mixed message" and give one example as it relates to corporate codes of ethics.

7. Restate in your own words the 10 principles listed in the chapter for quality codes of ethics.

8. Describe the following levels of codes of ethics:

theoretical level

practical level

currently attainable level

basic level

9. Summarize Robert E. Sweeney's five steps in the development of a viable corporate code of ethics.

    a.

    b.

    c.

    d.

    e.

10. Name three ways in which professional codes of ethics vary from corporate codes.

    a.

    b.

    c.

11. Discuss DeGeorge's four characteristics of a viable professional code:
    a.

    b.

    c.

    d.

12. Identify three potential limitations of professional codes.
    a.

    b.

    c.

13. List the three processes by which a professional code of ethics can be evaluated.
    a.

    b.

    c.

14. There are three ways in which government/public service codes of ethics are different from other codes. What are they?
    a.

    b.

    c.

15. Identify the three strengths and three weaknesses of government/public service codes as offered by the author.

strengths

weaknesses

16. List the "five most important points" from your reading.
a.

b.

c.

d.

e.

1.– Compare your list with those of other students.

2.– Compare, also, your textbook highlighting and margin notes.

3.– Justify to each other what appear to be the major points.

Applications

1. Write a paper on the subject of *Conflict of Interest and Codes of Ethics*. Include in your paper these topics:
   a. Introduction, including important definitions
   b. Examples of Conflict of Interest that may occur in the development and implementation of:
      1. Corporate Codes of Ethics
      2. Professional Codes of Ethics
      3. Government/Public Service Codes of Ethics
   c. Antidotes to Conflict of Interest in the development and implementation of:
      1. Corporate Codes of Ethics
      2. Professional Codes of Ethics
      3. Government/Public Service Codes of Ethics
   d. Conclusion, including personal observations.

2. Choose one of the major approaches to moral reasoning you have studied thus far in class. How would each of this approach answer the following questions:
   a. Is it ever morally right to violate a code of ethics?
   b. Is it ever morally right to overlook a violation of a code of ethics?
   c. Is it ever morally right to remain unacquainted with a code of ethics for which one is to be held responsible?

 **Cases**

Case 1. Lindsey is your county's zoning director. Jones Inc. has requested a change in zoning for one of its parcels of land. Usually, the re-zoning process takes several months at best. Jones Inc. cannot wait that long for financial reasons. Jones Inc. offers Lindsey $100 to "help push the papers through the bureaucratic process."

      a.   Should Lindsey refuse? Why or why not?
      b.   What if Jones Inc. gives Lindsey two tickets to a play at a local theater *after* the zoning change is completed in "appreciation for her efforts"?
      c.   What state/county Code sections apply, if any?

 Term Paper

Write a **CODE CRITIQUE:** Select a Corporate or Professional Code (such as the *Code of Professional Responsibility for Lawyers* or the *Code of Ethics for the Education Profession*) that is of particular interest to <u>you</u>. Write a critique of the Code in the following format:

I.   **INTRODUCTION**
Explain your knowledge of this business or profession. What experience or interest has drawn you to this area of pursuit? What do you hope to gain from undertaking this critique?

II.   **RESEARCH**
    A. Your textbook, *Business Ehics Applied*. See *Chapter 7* and *Appendix*.
    B. **Library Research** - Check your library.
        1. Consult the Internet, the card catalogue and-or one of the reference librarians on staff; <u>or</u>
        2. Contact a member of the business or profession you are researching, explain this assignment, and ask for a copy of his/her code.

III. **INTERVIEW(S)**
In an effort to learn more about the views of those involved in the business or profession you have selected, interview at least one individual regarding his/her views of the topics listed below. Your interview should be attached as an appendix to your critique. Be sure to include your interviewee's name.

IV. **CONTENT**
Your critique should cover the following areas, and should include your own viewpoint, as well as the viewpoint of your interviewee:
    A. What ethical issues are prevalent in this profession? Identify several.
    B. What ethical principles appear to be reflected in the code?
        1. Some examples of such principles might be honesty, fairness, justice, etc.

2. Examples of exactly how these principles are reflected in the code would be very appropriate.

C. Are these ethical principles adequate for this particular profession? Why or why not? Is the code in its entirety adequate for the profession it addresses? Why or why not?

D. What level does the code represent (basic, currently attainable, etc.)?

E. What have you learned, if anything, from undertaking this assignment, that might be useful to you in whatever business or profession you ultimately select?

Tips For Code Critique Writers From Former Students:

1. Choose a profession you are truly interested in; it makes all the difference in the world.
2. Get started as soon as possible, especially if you are writing away for information. Contact potential interviewees immediately.
3. Do more than one interview; this makes the assignment more interesting.
4. Don't be shy. Be eager and aggressive.
5. Take notes during the interview, even if you are using a recorder. Write them up right away.
6. For your interviews, go to people ready to start conversation.
7. Don't be afraid to sound ignorant if in fact you don't understand something. Ask questions.
8. Pay attention to conflicting statements; that's where your story may be.
9. Don't do this critique because you have to; think of ways to make it fun for you.
10. As you write, keep in mind how this process will be helpful to you later, even if you end up working in a different profession than the one about which you wrote.

Chapter VIII

DOING RIGHT IN BUSINESS

 Chief Learning Outcome: I understand the concept of corporations and professions and am able to discuss various moral theories as they apply to business decisions.

Learning Objectives

Given an opportunity to read and study this chapter, the student should be able to:

1. Explain the meaning of all Key Concepts and the Major Terms and Names from the chapter and describe their relevance to the study of applied ethics.
2. Recall Aristotle's view of commerce?
3. Summarize the impact that St. Benedict's view of "work" had on the world.
4. Recall the role of the first middle class.
5. Summarize the meaning of contractual "quid pro quo."
6. Distinguish the difference between a "moral obligation" and a "contract."
7. Recall Hobbes and Locke's rules on acquiring property.
8. Recall how Luther impacted the idea of work.
9. Explain the author's definition of the fundamental "capitalist" act.
10. Recognize Adam Smith's most memorable accomplishment.
11. List the virtues presupposed by the free market system.
12. List three work maxims espoused by Franklin.
13. Summarize the nature of a "for profit corporation."
14. Recall the parties and roles of those involved in the corporation.
15. Explain how mutual funds affect ownership of the corporation.
16. Recall how Malthus' grim demographics influence the conduct of business.
17. State the conclusion D. Ricardo reached concerning Mathus' theory and the law of labor supply and demand?
18. Recognize G.W.F. Hegel's three-point succession view.
19. Summarize Marx's theory.
20. List some of the claims that help to define a profession.
21. Distinguish between "market ethics" and "professional ethics."

KEY CONCEPTS

For-profit Corporation is a venture financed by investors (the people who put their money into the venture, at the outset or later on) for the purpose of making more money, getting a return on investment (ROI) as great or greater than they could get in any other allotment of their money.

Contract is an agreement – a *quid pro quo*, mutual promising of something in exchange for something else – to mutual performance of some specific commitments.

Trade is the willing exchange with another for the purpose of advancing one's own interests; it is the fundamental "capitalist act."

Categorical imperatives are rules that always define appropriate conduct; e.g., "Don't kill anyone, ever."

Hypothetical imperatives are rules for what to do in order to achieve certain goals; e.g., "Eat an apple a day to stay healthy."

A **profession** is, briefly, an occupational group distinguished from others by possession of a constellation of properties, more or less central to its operations.

A **fiduciary obligation** is a duty that professionals have toward their clients to make each decision for the client's best interests and welfare, not the professional's own.

Major Terms and Names

(These may also appear in the questions below.)

1. the bottom line
2. St. Benedict
3. vocation
4. Guilds and Burghers
5. bourgeoisie
6. private property
7. Thomas Hobbes
8. society
9. John Locke
10. Civil Government
11. entitlement
12. Martin Luther
13. Bentham
14. hedonism
15. the Common Good
16. utilitarian calculus
17. Adam Smith

18. altruism
19. capitalist act
20. supply and demand
21. free enterprise
22. invisible hand
23. liberty
24. Benjamin Franklin
25. responsibility
26. return on investment (ROI)
27. limited liability
28. mercantilist
29. "private sector" corporation
30. ownership
31. stock
32. principals
33. agent
34. fiduciary obligation
35. beneficiary
36. dividends
37. shareholders
38. Board of Directors
39. mutual funds
40. bonds
41. broker
42. Thomas Malthus
43. Essay on Population
44. division of labor
45. David Ricardo
46. productivity
47. Charles Dickens
48. Karl Marx
49. moral response
50. Industrial Revolution
51. aesthetic
52. G.W.F. Hegel
53. thesis
54. antithesis
55. synthesis
56. ruling class
57. proletariat
58. disillusionment of the workers
59. dictatorship of the proletariat
60. heavily capitalized manufacturing
61. mass production
62. Iron Law of Wages
63. labor unions
64. internal constituencies
65. external constituencies
66. profession
67. fiduciary
68. market ethic
69. professional ethic

Review Questions

1. What was Aristotle's view of commerce?

2. What impact did St. Benedict have on the world view of "work"?

3. Who made up the first "middle" class and what role did they play in commerce?

4. What was meant by contractual "quid pro quo"?

5. What is the difference between a "moral obligation" and a "contract"?

6. How did Hobbes and Locke claim people could acquire property? What were the exceptions to their rules if any?

7. How did Luther impact the idea of work?

8.   What does the author define as the fundamental "capitalist" act? Explain.

9.   What was Adam Smith's most memorable accomplishment according to the author?

10.   What are the virtues presupposed by the free market system?

11.   List three of the maxims of the work ethic espoused by Franklin.

   a.

   b.

   c.

12.   Describe the nature of a "for-profit corporation."

13.   List the parties involved in the makeup of a corporation and explain their roles.

14. How do mutual funds affect ownership of the corporation?

15. How did Malthus's grim demographics influence the conduct of business?

16. What conclusion did D. Ricardo reach concerning Mathus's theory and the law of labor supply and demand?

17. Define G.W.F. Hegel's three point succession view.
    a.

    b.

    c.

18. Summarize Marx's theory.

19. List some of the claims that help to define a profession.

20. Compare/contrast "market ethics" and "professional ethics."

21. List the "five most important points" from your reading.

a.

b.

c.

d.

e.

1.– Compare your list with those of other students.

2.– Compare, also, your textbook highlighting and margin notes.

3.– Justify to each other what appear to be the major points.

 ## Applications

1. Take two of Benjamin Franklin's four maxims and apply them to a business today. Do they work as well now as they did in Franklin's time?

2. Assume you are the CEO of a private corporation needing funds, and you are considering the advantages and disadvantages of becoming a publicly held corporation. What recommendation will you make to your board of directors? What is your rationale?

 ## Cases

Case 1. The economic pressure on York International was great. Foreign imports had significantly reduced their share of the domestic automobile market to the point where York's survival as a corporation depended on the success of the newly designed Jupiter. The normal three years it took from the initial concept to the finished product had been squeezed to 18 months. Market tests indicated that the Jupiter had successfully anticipated new consumer preferences, and York International was eight months to a year ahead of its foreign competitors. In fact, production had already begun and the first Jupiters would be in the showrooms in a couple of months.

It was under these circumstances that the CEO of York and a handful of top executives were faced with an agonizing decision: A memo from the chief design engineer of the Jupiter revealed that a design flaw would cause the air bags to fail in approximately one out of every 250 head-on crashes. The mistake could be corrected, but it would cost millions to retool and would delay sales for at least six months.

After the top legal and marketing executives were consulted, the options were quickly reduced to two: First, continue production, re-establish market share and the profitability of the company, and then pay generous settlements if (when?) suits are brought against the company. Second, recall the Jupiter, discontinue production during retooling and almost certainly face the demise of York International. The CEO of York chose the former.

Three years later, after York had re-established itself as a viable company, the CEO of York read the following statement at a news conference prior to beginning his five- to 10-year sentence at the federal penitentiary:

"While I have broken the law, my conscience is clear. We had a union contract and the livelihood of thousands of employees under that contract was on the line three years ago. Life is tragic. Either option was sure to cause great pain. My critics will retort: Human life is priceless; no purely economic advantage will ever outweigh the loss of even a single life. But that is simply not true. First, there is no such thing as a purely economic advantage. When 10,000 employees lose their jobs, it is statistically certain that there will be one or two suicides, hundreds of divorces, and the neglect or abuse of thousands of children. Second, our economic system continually engages in cost-benefit analysis. We trade tobacco subsidies for cancer deaths; the reduction of air traffic controllers for airline accidents; and political expediency for the lives of famine-stricken children in foreign countries when their governments vote against us in the United Nations. My decision was no more immoral than any of these and the countless others that all politicians and business executives make at least once in their lives."

a. Was the CEO of York International correct when he said that there is no such thing as a purely economic advantage? Is he correct to suggest that all major economic decisions inevitably involve matters of life and death?

b. The CEO's second argument seems to be open to the objection that "two wrongs don't make a right." But if we make such an objection, does moral consistency demand that we also become actively involved in correcting the other abuses of economic power mentioned above?

c. If the CEO of York were a conscientious utilitarian, how might he have acted? A conscientious Kantian? A conscientious communitarian?

Chapter IX

EMPLOYEE RIGHTS AND RESPONSIBILITIES

Chief Learning Outcome: I understand employee and employer responsibilities in both legal and ethical dimensions.

 Learning Objectives

Given an opportunity to read and study this chapter, the student should be able to:

1. Explain the meaning of all Key Concepts and the Major Terms and Names from the chapter and describe their relevance to the study of applied ethics.
2. List the five types of rights employees have.
3. Define: nepotism, cronyism, discrimination, affirmative action and quotas.
4. Recall the Supreme Court's conclusions as to sex stereotyping in the Price Waterhouse Case.
5. Summarize the "lay-off" decision Bill Lee of Duke Power made and his reasoning.
6. Recount the pros and cons of affirmative action.
7. List the advantages to be gained by a diverse workplace.
8. List the elements of the three-way test used to justify employer monitoring of an employee.
9. Recall workplace conditions caused by substance abuse.
10. Summarize the effect of the federal laws on alcoholism in the workplace.
11. Recall the status of HIV/AIDS testing.
12. Summarize the impact OSHA has had on businesses and industry.
13. State how women of childbearing years can be adversely affected by employment in certain chemical factories.
14. Recall the "mommy track" *pros* and *cons.*
15. State what is meant by "dignity" in the workplace.
16. Describe the two primary types of sexual harassment.
17. List the five ways McCall justifies employees' participation in decision-making.
18. Recall Norman Bowie's classic definition and set of criteria for the moral justification of blowing the whistle.
19. Summarize Pat Werhane's employee rights and obligations.
20. Identify and explain the four virtues set forth in the author's "integrity curriculum."

KEY CONCEPTS

Non-Discrimination means the corporation shall adhere to fair laws in hiring and promoting, with no discrimination among workers that is not clearly related to the job.

Employee rights direct that the corporation respect the employee's public and private rights, especially the right to privacy.

Employee welfare requests the corporation to protect the health and safety of the employees, and maintain a healthy and accident-free workplace.

Employee dignity means that the corporation shall maintain a workplace that protects and nurtures dignity, free from physical or psychological harassment, free from degrading stereotypes.

Employee integrity maintains that the corporation provides channels through which employees may question and criticize company decisions and policy.

Mutual responsibility requires that the corporation exercise responsibility over the areas which it controls (the physical conditions of the workspace, the monitoring devices and policies in place), while the employees take responsibility for that portion of the work that is within their control.

Major Terms and Names

(These may also appear in the questions below.)

1. prejudice
2. nepotism
3. cronyism
4. discrimination
5. Equal Protection Act of 1963
6. Title VII of the Civil Rights Act of 1964
7. 1972 Equal Employment Opportunity Act
8. Age Discrimination in Employment Act (ADEA) of 1967
9. Americans with Disabilities Act (ADA) of 1990
10. affirmative action
11. quota
12. Equal Employment Opportunity Commission
13. Diane Harris
14. stereotyping
15. sex stereotyping
16. reverse discrimination
17. Proposition 209
18. melting pot

19. testing and monitoring
20. supervision
21. right of privacy
22. trust
23. lie detector test
24. three-way test
25. substance abuse
26. hair sampling
27. genetic data
28. creaming
29. Human Immunodeficiency Virus (HIV)
30. Acquired Immunodeficiency Disease Syndrome (AIDS)
31. employment at will
32. Adam Smith
33. wages-and-hours laws
34. workers' compensation laws
35. protection of health and safety
36. Occupational Safety and Health Administration (OSHA)
37. asbestos
38. mutagen
39. teratogens
40. repetitive stress injury (RSI)
41. wellness programs
42. mommy tracks
43. sexual harassment
44. quid pro quo
45. hostile environment
46. reasonable person
47. diversity
48. workplace decision-making
49. John McCall
50. Bolivar Project
51. blowing the whistle
52. Norman Bowie
53. Challenger
54. Patricia Werhane
55. employee rights
56. employee obligations
57. United Technologies Corporation
58. mutual responsibility
59. integrity curriculum
60. wisdom
61. courage
62. patience
63. justice

1. What types of rights do employees have?

2. Discuss the following:
   a. nepotism

   b. cronyism

   c. discrimination

      1) affirmative action

      2) quota

3. What were the Supreme Court's conclusions as to sex stereotyping in the Price Waterhouse Case?

4. What "lay-off" decision did Bill Lee of Duke Power make and what was his reasoning?

5.   Is "affirmative action" justified? Give pro and con justifications.
     a. Pro

     b. Con

6.   What are the advantages to be gained by a diverse workplace?

7.   List and explain the components of the monitoring three-way test.

8.   Name the workplace conditions created by substance abuse.

9.   What is the effect of the ADA on alcoholism in the workplace?

10. What is the status of HIV and AIDS testing?

11.   How has OSHA affected businesses and industry?

12.   How can women of childbearing years be adversely affected by their employment in certain chemical factories?

13.   Discuss thoroughly the "mommy track" *pros* and *cons.*

14.   What is meant by "dignity" in the workplace?

15.   Define sexual harassment and discuss its two major categories?

16.   List the five ways employee participation in decision-making can be justified according to McCall.
    a.

    b.

    c.

    d.

    e.

17.   Give Bowie's classic definition and set of criteria for the moral justification of blowing the whistle.

18.   Compare/contrast Pat Werhane's employee rights and obligations.

19.   List and explain the four virtues set forth in the author's "integrity curriculum."

a.

b.

c.

d.

20.   List the "five most important points" from your reading.

a.

b.

c.

d.

e.

      1.– Compare your list with those of other students.

      2.– Compare, also, your textbook highlighting and margin notes.

      3.– Justify to each other what appear to be the major and why.

Applications

1.   Do you agree with the author that AIDS testing in the workplace is especially problematic? Why or why not? On what general moral principles do you base your position?

2.   Some employers attempt to restrict the actions of their employees outside of the workplace for such activities as smoking, drinking alcohol and sky diving. Do you believe such restrictions are ethically permissible? Why or why not? On what general moral principles do you base your position?

3.   Give an example from your own knowledge and-or your own personal experience of someone who has achieved despite obstacles of prejudice.

4.   If you were the president of a company, would you institute any policies to keep the workplace free of sexual harassment? If so, what would they be? On what general moral principles do you base your position?

5.   Find a newspaper and-or magazine article referencing some aspect of discrimination in the workplace as discussed in the chapter. Study the article and answer the following questions:

   a.   What are the moral issues presented?
   b.   Does the information in the article give rise to any conflicts of interest?
   c.   What are they? What tipped you off to the conflict? Do you think it would be important for the conflict to be resolved? Why or why not?
   d.   What was the outcome? Do you agree or disagree? Give your reasons.

 Cases

Case 1. Polly Green has been a personal secretary to the First Lady for the past three years. During this time Polly has observed what she considers to be insincerity on the part of the First Lady with regard to her interest in social causes. Polly feels the public should know of this hypocrisy and has contacted a publisher to find out how much she might be paid for her story.

Case 2. Molly Marble is a nurse at Centerville General Hospital. Molly has noticed that her best friend, Nan Nervous, has been behaving strangely at work lately. Molly suspects that Nan may be under the influence of drugs or alcohol. Nan has just been transferred to the intensive care unit. She will now be caring for the critically ill on the midnight shift.

Case 3. Tom Tattler is an engineering student entering his senior year at State University. Tom was selected to participate in an internship program at a prestigious engineering firm. The internship provides valuable practical experience as well as the possibility of a job offer. While working on an assignment at the firm, Tom discovers what appears to be an oversight, which if allowed to remain uncorrected would have serious ramifications on the environment. When Tom alerts his supervisor, Tom is told "not to worry," that this has been done at the client's insistence, and that the EPA has already approved the plan. Tom is concerned that the plan, if implemented, will be destructive to the environment, killing all aquatic life within a 20-mile radius.

For each case:
a. List as many moral reasons as you can surrounding the situation.
b. Apply Norman Bowie's criteria for moral justification of whistle-blowing and conclude whether each subject would be justified in blowing the whistle. Explain your answer.

Chapter X

CUSTOMERS, COMMUNITY AND WORLD

Chief Learning Outcome: I can recognize ethical issues in the modern business world and apply moral reasoning to them.

 Learning Objectives

Given an opportunity to read and study this chapter, the student should be able to:

1. Explain the meaning of all Key Concepts and the Major Terms and Names from the chapter and describe their relevance to the study of applied ethics.
2. List the five duties a corporation has to those outside the corporation.
3. Recall how the manufacturer of any product is accountable to the consumer.
4. Recall the message sent by the jury in McDonald's Hot Coffee Case.
5. Summarize the bases for and the outcomes of the *Hopkins vs. Dow Corning* Case.
6. Recall two convictions we should try to inculcate as practical guides for our behavior.
7. Recall the manufacturer's responsibility as to packaging and labeling.
8. State the three things the author identifies as "rules for doing one's consumer duty."
9. Explain why we should be concerned about the content of advertisement to children and teens.
10. Restate the difference between the "stakeholder" and the "stockholder" corporate models.
11. Discuss two of the most common concerns of a community as to business.
12. Restate the responsibility a business has to the community for plant/business closings?
13. Recall the responsibility of citizenry and local governments to maintain the welfare of their community.
14. Summarize the meaning of insider trading and the two applicable theories.
15. Explain why it was necessary to enact the Foreign Corrupt Practices Act of 1977.
16. Summarize the responsibility American corporations should have for working conditions in developing countries.
17. Summarize the environmental stewardship responsibility of corporations.
18. Recall the "responsibility perspective" outlined for corporations.

KEY CONCEPTS

Quality of product and service implies that products should be safe, durable, and beautiful; the services should be promptly and cheerfully performed; what is done should be done right the first time. At the least, the company should be able to stand behind anything it makes or does.

Veracity (truth and sensitivity) should be present; first, in the representation of the corporation and its product; and second, in the right and duty of the consumer to exercise prudence in making choices of what to buy.

Good citizenship requires that in all the communities in which the corporation functions, the corporation is to operate with candor and cooperation with the government(s) and governmental agencies and community organizations.

Consistency in the application of moral codes and standards, establishes a pattern of reliability in the corporation. It is the job of the multinational corporation in the first instance to establish what its position will be regarding everything from bribes to working conditions, and to stick with its position.

Stewardship in conducting business in the environment, advocates that the corporation seek to reduce or eliminate pollution, preferably by recycling its elements; conserve resources; avoid cost-cutting at the expense of environmental protection and seek always to respect whole biosphere, the entire interlocking system of topsoil, plant life, oceans and ocean life, and the composition of the atmosphere itself, including the ozone layer, seen as one interdependent living system.

Major Terms and Names

(These may also appear in the questions below.)

1.   social contract for business
2.   consumer
3.   customer
4.   user
5.   warranty
6.   duty not to harm
7.   due care
8.   negligence
9.   contract law
10. caveat emptor
11. Ralph Nader
12. *Unsafe At Any Speed*
13. Pinto Case
14. criminal charges
15. sport utility vehicle (SUV)

16. strict liability
17. Food and Drug Administration
18. The Tylenol case
19. product stewardship
20. product paternalism
21. craftsman's ethic
22. consumer patience
23. truthfulness
24. marketing
25. reasonable person
26. packaging and labeling
27. game of salesmanship
28. duty of prudence
29. brand preference
30. John Kenneth Galbraith
31. dependence effect
32. Federal Trade Commission Act
33. Borg-Warner
34. stockholder model
35. stakeholder model
36. honesty
37. insider trading
38. fiduciary
39. misappropriation theory
40. the "tipper-tippee" theory
41. The Savings and Loan Collapse
42. Charles Keating
43. Ernst & Young
44. International Corporate Ethics
45. the "new social contract"
46. bribery
47. extortion
48. Foreign Corrupt Practices Act of 1977
49. grease
50. Worker's Rights
51. sweatshops
52. biosphere
53. mutual responsibility
54. quality
55. citizenship
56. consistency
57. stewardship
58. a responsibility perspective
59. community
60. foresight

Review Questions

1.	What are the duties a corporation has to those outside the corporation? List the five duties named by the author.

	a.

	b.

	c.

	d.

	e.

2.	How is the manufacturer of any product accountable to the consumer?

3.	The jury in the McDonald's Hot Coffee Case was said to be sending a message to fast-food establishments. What was it?

4.	What was the bases for and the outcomes of the *Hopkins vs. Dow Corning* Case?

5.	The author names two convictions that should be inculcated as practical guides for behavior. Name and define both.

	a.

	b.

6.	What is the manufacturer's responsibility as to packaging and labeling?

7.   List the three things the author identifies as "rules for doing one's consumer duty."

8.   Should we be concerned about the content of advertisement to children and teens and why?

9.   Compare/contrast the stakeholder and the stockholder corporate models.

10.   Name and discuss two of the most common concerns of any community about corporate behavior.
          a.

          b.

11.   What responsibility does business have to the community for plant and business closings, if any?

12.   Do local citizens and their government maintain responsibility for the welfare of their town or city? If so, what might they do to ensure social responsibility on the part of corporations?

13.   Define insider trading and the two applicable theories.

14.   Why was it necessary for Congress to pass the Foreign Corrupt Practices Act of 1977?

15.   What responsibility should American corporations have for working conditions in developing countries?

16.   Discuss the environmental stewardship responsibility of corporations.

17.   The author formulates a "responsibility perspective" for corporations. List and explain its three general propositions.

18. List the "five most important points" from your reading.

a.

b.

c.

d.

e.

1.– Compare your list with those of other students.

2.– Compare, also, your textbook highlighting and margin notes.

3.– Justify to each other what appear to be the major points.

Applications

1.   If we are trying to ensure quality in our manufactured products, it is hard to imagine a less efficient, or more corrosive, mechanism than civil liability for negligence. It requires huge public expenditure as cases drag through the public courts; it consumes the time, energy, minds and souls of the people involved, who can think of nothing but the fate of their lawsuit for years at a stretch; and in the end, whatever money is transferred from the manufacturer to pay the judgment of the court goes largely for costs and fees for the lawyers on both sides.

a. What would be a better policy?

b. How about a government agency in charge of Setting Things Right (or some such title) that heard all cases of alleged negligence and decided on the basis of general common sense and the advice of a few ethicists? State the advantages and disadvantages of such a proposal.

2.   Find a newspaper article concerning environmental and-or working conditions of an American corporation in a developing country.

a. What are the moral issues presented? Identify as many as you can.

b. Does the information in the article give rise to any conflicts of interest? Identify them.

c. Identify any fallacies.

3.   It would have been a good thing if Morton Thiokol and NASA had listened to Roger Boisjoly before the launch of the Challenger and the disaster that followed.

a. After the disaster, when nothing could save the astronauts, was it right for him to wash all the dirty linen in front of the U.S. Congress?

b. Should he have helped maintain a united front to the world? Argue both sides.

 **Cases**

Case 1. At 12:07 a.m. on the morning of March 24, 1989, the 987-foot supertanker *Exxon Valdez* ran aground on Bligh Reef in Prince William Sound, Alaska. The impact tore open 8 of the 11 cargo tanks, causing the largest oil spill in U.S. history. The approximately 11-million gallons of Alaskan-crude oil that spilled into the waters of the Sound killed and injured fish, birds, mammals, and a variety of other forms of marine life, habitats, and resources.

After the *Exxon Valdez* hit Bligh Reef, the response was far short of that called for in the contingency plan. Promised cleanup equipment was not available. The barge that was assigned to spill response had been damaged and was not loaded with the required equipment. Reloading the barge was made more difficult by the fact that one man had to run both a crane and forklift. Even locating the response equipment was made difficult by the covering of snow that obscured it. The result was that the loading and deployment took four times longer than called for in the contingency plan. Skimmers and booms did not arrive at the site until nearly 18 hours after the grounding. This was three times longer than called for in the plan. At 70 hours, a point at which the contingency plan stated that a spill of more than 200,000 barrels would be cleaned up, no more than 3,000 barrels had been recovered. Then the weather turned bad. The wind quickly spread the slick from one of eight-mile length to a 40-mile-long disaster for Prince William Sound - a disaster from which many experts predicted a very slow recovery. Prince William Sound is located on the south-central Alaskan coast. It is part of a remote, pristine fjord/estuary-type ecosystem containing important natural resources. At least five species of threatened or endangered marine mammals frequent the area at certain times of the year. The Sound is one of the largest, undeveloped marine ecosystems in the United States, with a population of only about 6,000 people in scattered towns and villages.

The economy of the Prince William Sound area is based on utilization of its abundant natural resources, which include commercial fishing, recreation, subsistence or personal-use fishing and hunting, logging, and oil transportation. The Sound supports major commercial salmon and herring fisheries, as well as smaller fisheries for king crab, shrimp, and halibut. Port Valdez, located in the northeastern portion of Prince William Sound, is the southern terminus of the Trans-Alaska Pipeline.

On December 9, 1989, the state and federal governments signed an agreement with the Exxon Corporation to settle criminal charges and civil damage claims in exchange for a payment of $1.1025-billion.

Additional Questions:

a. Should the citizens and the local government adjoining Prince William Sound have established any ordinances governing the corporate responsibility of shippers passing by their waters? What type protections could they have built in to their ordinances?

b. What responsibilities do shipping companies have to the communities onshore from their shipping lanes?

Chapter XI

COMMUNICATIONS IN COMMERCE

💡 **Chief Learning Outcome: I can recognize ethical issues in communications in the technology era and apply moral reasoning to them.**

 Learning Objectives

Given an opportunity to read and study this chapter, the student should be able to:

1. Explain the meaning of all Key Concepts and the Major Terms and Names from the chapter and describe their relevance to the study of applied ethics.
2. Describe the role of "official" communicator, the "professional" communicator, and the "spin doctor."
3. Explain how the untruthful communicator might place the employer or the client at risk.
4. Define the purpose of communication.
5. Summarize the federal law regarding copying of computer software.
6. Identify two principles each from five sections of the EDUCOM code of ethics.
7. Describe the vulnerability of our computer record keeping systems.
8. Describe what is made available to the public under the Freedom of Information Act.
9. Discuss the history of libel law in the United States.
10. Recall additional questions that need to be answered when one believes it is sometimes ethical to do things as a business professional that would otherwise be considered unethical or immoral.
11. Recall two examples of when the notion of "special license for journalists to break the normal rules" has resulted in the firing of corporate employees.
12. Recall the message sent in the Food Lion case.
13. Name two new issues raised by the advent of computer imaging.
14. Describe the status of "commercial" speech.
15. Summarize the author's position that truthfulness is the "pivotal idea" in professional communications.
16. Explain "the dilemma of truth" and the "dilemma of zeal."

 ## KEY CONCEPTS

Truth is objectively accurate statements, always applicable.

Lying is not telling the truth, including verbal and non-verbal expressions; one of the acts forbidden by the Ten Commandments and The Koran and by every court of law.

Plagiarism is the action whereby one appropriates another's writings or works or art and makes use of them as one's own; implied is the notion that by so doing one is "stealing" original work produced by another.

Private property consists of goods, land, structures and intellectual assets (music, books, computer software) owned by private individuals or corporations.

Professional ethics consists of the standards or codes of conduct adopted formally by a group of persons practicing the same vocation.

Right of privacy is the notion, explicit in some state constitutions, that each individual has a legal right prohibiting invasion of home or personal life.

Situational ethics is determining what is right or good solely on the basis of the momentary context; implying that what is right or good today in this situation may not be right tomorrow in another set of circumstances.

Times vs. Sullivan is a landmark U.S. Supreme Court ruling involving libel law in which the private lives of public persons fell under the concept of the general public's right to know and the news media's right to obtain information.

 ## Major Terms and Names

(These may also appear in the questions below.)

1. professional communicator
2. conflict
3. spin doctor
4. dishonesty
5. final test
6. fraud
7. libel
8. First Amendment to the U.S. Constitution
9. cyber world
10. Adam C. Powell III
11. altered images
12. computer ethics
13. intellectual property

14. copyright law
15. EDUCOM
16. computer-hacking
17. integrity
18. Internet
19. Freedom of Information (FOI) Act
20. interactive software
21. actual malice
22. American Society of Newspaper Editors (ASNE)
23. situational ethics
24. commercial speech
25. bait-and-switch advertising
26. *caveat emptor*
27. public relations
28. Public Relations Society of America (PRSA)
29. dilemmas of truth
30. dilemmas of zeal

 Review Questions

1. Describe the role of:
   "official" communicator

   "professional" communicator

2. Explain how the untruthful communicator might place the employer or the client at risk.

3. Describe the role of the "spin doctor."

4. Define the purpose of communication and its final test.

5. Summarize the federal law regarding copying of computer software.

6. Identify two principles each from the following sections of the EDUCOM code of ethics:

Software and Intellectual Rights

Commercial software

Shareware software

Freeware software

Public Domain

7. Describe the vulnerability of computer record keeping systems.

8. What is to be made available to the public under the Freedom of Information Act?

9. Outline the history of libel law in the United States.

10. According to the author, additional questions must be answered when one believes it sometimes is ethical to do things as a businessperson/professional that would otherwise be considered unethical/immoral. What are those questions and why should they be asked?

11. Two examples of when the notion of "special license for journalists to break the normal rules" resulted in the firing of corporate employees are:
    a.

    b.

12. In the case of *Food Lion vs. ABC*, what message was the jury sending to all journalists?

13. Two new issues raised by the advent of computer imaging are:
    a.

    b.

14. Describe the constitutional status of commercial speech.

15. Summarize the author's position that truthfulness is the "pivotal idea" in professional communications.

16. Explain and discuss the following:
a. dilemma of truth

b. dilemma of zeal

17. List the "five most important points" from your reading.
a.

b.

c.

d.

e.

1.– Compare your list with those of other students.

2.– Compare, also, your textbook highlighting and margin notes.

3.– Justify to each other what appear to be the major points.

Applications

1.   Do you think the media play a significant role in influencing our view of communications in commerce? Explain your answer and, if possible, include examples.

2.   Can you recall a time when someone attempted to justify a "professional lie?" If so, answer the following questions:
   a. What was the argument given to justify the lie?
   b. Did you agree or disagree with the argument? Why?
   c. Did the argument contain any fallacies? If so, what were they?
   d. What general moral principle(s) did the person seem to be relying upon in support of the conclusion that the lie was ethically permissible?
   e. At what stage of Kohlberg's theory of moral development did the person appear to be functioning? Explain your answer.

3.   Imagine that you are starting a newspaper in your community. Are there any journalistic goals or ideals that you would want to establish in setting the tone for the ethical climate at your newspaper? What would they be? On what general moral principles would you base such decisions?

4.   Answer No. 3 with regard to:
   a. a public relations firm;
   b. an advertising agency.

5.   What is it that makes a story "newsworthy"? Consider some definitions from the literature and try your hand at creating such a story.

6.   If you are interviewing a person for a story you are writing, and the person keeps asking you if you "understand," "agree," "see my point of view," and you really don't but you want to keep the person talking, is it wrong to pretend to agree, for the sake of the story? Why or why not?

Cases

Case 1. An editor, back in the newsroom, may insist that the reporter bring her a detailed story about the bank teller who embezzled $50,000 to spend on his girlfriend and on drugs. That editor does not see the embezzler's children, who are devastated by the arrest and will be impacted greatly by printed descriptions of their father's illicit love nest. Contrarily, the reporter may want to use all the facts he has garnered, while the editor may feel an obligation to exercise restraint.

There is little dispute over the news media's duty to report the arrest of the embezzler. There is considerable debate, however, over the ethics of including colorful details, such as descriptions of the sexy lingerie the bank teller bought for the girlfriend. While those journalists whom Meyer identifies as First Amendment fundamentalists would not hesitate to publish every detail they could get, an even greater number feel an obligation to consider the entire situation before deciding.

   a. List as many moral issues as you can think of surrounding the situation described.

b. Apply one or more approaches to moral reasoning. Each time you apply an approach, be sure to include the following:
   1. What steps would be undertaken with that approach, and how would those steps apply specifically to the case?
   2. Based on applying the steps and showing how they would "work" in this particular case, what might be the ultimate resolution?
   3. Write at least one syllogism in response to the dilemma that the case presents. Make sure each syllogism reflects a general moral principle embodied in the approach to moral reasoning that you have applied.

Chapter XII

DECISION-MAKING IN PUBLIC SERVICE

Chief Learning Outcome: I can apply theories of moral reasoning to evaluate public decisions and those who make them.

Learning Objectives

Given an opportunity to read and study this chapter, the student should be able to:

1. Explain the meaning of all Key Concepts and the Major Terms and Names from the chapter and describe their relevance to the study of applied ethics.
2. Explain the quote from Thomas Jefferson: "When a man assumes a public trust, he should consider himself as public property."
3. Recall the general duties of sound governance.
4. List the competing values and interests public officials face as they approach decision-making.
5. Summarize the five steps to principled reasoning offered by the Josephson model for decision-making.
6. Recall three of the "most important official virtues," as put forward by Kathryn Denhardt.
7. Recall significant differences between the types of dilemmas faced as a candidate and those faced as a politician in office, as identified by Walter Lippman.
8. Recall types of ethical misconduct occurring in the '90s.
9. Explain the need for Campaign Finance Reform.
10. Explain "Sunshine" laws.

KEY CONCEPTS

Competing values and interests of official decisions involve the **Constitution** of the United States and, where applicable, the Constitution of a state, the **laws** of the land, certain **regulations or rules,** prescribed **guidelines** within the regulations, **precedents** and **procedures,** including those involved in an official **audit,** as well as *specific* **codes of ethics** and any prevailing **court rulings** of the U.S. Supreme Court or the federal appeals court in a given region of the nation, and finally, the **governing culture** of the office – the dominant values around which most decisions are made.

Duties of Sound Governance are **prudence** – the wise management of resources for the benefit of the whole including the virtues of foresight and frugality; **courage of conscience** – the quality of character recognizes compromises and does not hesitate to act on a balance of idealism and realism; and **truth-telling** – official telling of the *whole truth* to appropriate authority.

Moral Foundations of Public Administration are honor, benevolence, and justice.

 Major Terms and Names

(These may also appear in the questions below.)

1. High calling
2. Abraham Lincoln
3. Richard Nixon
4. Watergate
5. Wilbur Mills
6. John Tower
7. Gary Hart
8. Jimmy Carter
9. Josephson Institute of Ethics
10. "Golden Kantian Consequentialism"
11. principled reasoning
12. Kathryn G. Denhardt
13. honor
14. benevolence
15. justice
16. *Ethical Frontiers in Public Management*
17. politician
18. statesman
19. Walter Lippman
20. conflicts of interest
21. Florida Commission on Ethics
22. President Bill Clinton
23. Thomas Jefferson
24. Office of Government Ethics
25. campaign finance reform
26. Uniform disclosure
27. bundled
28. "Who Gave It, Who Got It" disclosure law
29. Revolving door
30. Independent Counsel
31. The Sunshine Law
32. Governor Reubin Askew

❓ Review Questions

1. What are the general duties of sound governance?
   a.

   b.

   c.

2. Name the competing values and interest that public officials face as they approach decision-making.
   a.
   b.
   c.
   d.
   e.
   f.
   g.
   h.
   i.

3. Summarize the *Five Steps to Principled Reasoning* offered by the Josephson model for decision-making:
   Clarify

   Evaluate

   Decide

   Implement

4. List three of the "most important official virtues," as put forward by Denhardt.

    a.

    b.

    c.

5. Identify Walter Lippman's three significant differences between the kinds of dilemmas faced as a candidate and those faced as a politician in office.

    a.

    b.

    c.

6. Discuss three types of ethical misconduct listed by the author as occurring in the '90s.

    a.

    b.

    c.

7. Explain the quote from Thomas Jefferson: "When a man assumes a public trust, he should consider himself as public property."

8. Discuss campaign finance problems and reform.

9. What is meant by a "Sunshine Law"?

10. List the "five most important points" from your reading.
   a.

   b.

   c.

   d.

   e.

      1.– Compare your list with those of other students.
      2.– Compare, also, your textbook highlighting and margin notes.
      3.– Justify to each other what appear to be the major points.

☞ Applications

1. The author asks, "Does taking the oath of office for public officials thereafter demand a high standard, one of avoiding the appearance as well as the actuality of unethical behavior?" What do you think? Discuss the reasons for your answers.

2. Research and summarize the law in your state regarding disclosure of campaign contributions.

3. Would you classify the campaign contribution law in your state as morally responsible? Why or why not?

4. Do you think Congress needs to address campaign reform. Write a letter to one of your elected officials expressing your opinion. You need not mail it.

5. Do you think the media play a significant role in influencing our attitudes and views regarding public officials? Explain your answer and include examples.

6. Find newspaper and-or magazine articles referencing questionable ethics on the part of a public servant. Study them, and answer the following:
   a. What is the main ethical issue presented?
   b. What resolution of the issue is suggested by applying these steps?
      1) Apply the Josephson model, *Five Steps to Principled Reasoning* to the issue.

2) Apply the Denhardt model to the issue. What resolution is suggested by applying these three virtues?
3) Apply one of the approaches to moral reasoning and explain your reasoning.

 Cases

Case 1. In 1974-75 President Nixon "stonewalled" congressional inquiries, participated in a "coverup" about illegal activities and lied in public statements about his actions. When discovered, he resigned. In 1998, President Clinton "stonewalled" congressional inquiries as well as federal prosecutors about allegedly illegal activities, conducted a "coverup" of his actions, lied to the public and *allegedly* did not tell the truth to civil and grand juries.

    a. Compare the two presidents' responses to inquiries. What was similar? What was different?
    b. What was the difference between the unlawful and immoral aspects of each?
    c. What might have happened in each president's situation if he would had applied Denhardt's three principles?
    d. What might have happened if each president had applied Josephson's model for decision-making?

NOTES